"What is God *really* like? Much of the stress and anxiety in our lives can be traced back to the misconceptions we have about our Heavenly Father. Bill Ritchie's book will help you to know God as he actually is. He'll help you move beyond 'religion' to a more satisfying relationship with God."

> Rick Warren, pastor
> Saddleback Valley Community Church
> Mission Viejo, California

"It's time for the hidden hurting who were wounded as a result of a disappointing father relationship, to 'be transformed by the renewing of your mind.' God delights in offering his children fresh starts and second chances. *A Dad Who Will Love You* will guide you to Truth—to your loving Heavenly Father who is the only Perfect Dad, who longs for a relationship with you."

> Dr. John C. Maxwell, senior pastor
> Skyline Wesleyan Church
> Lemon Grove, California

"Fatherhood is under siege today by the forces of darkness. Bill Ritchie plainly shows us what a perfect Dad looks like and shows us the image of God as our Heavenly Father in a very loving and practical light. I commend this book to the reader. It is well-thought out and gently written—holding out the promise of tremendous blessing and healing for many."

> Mike MacIntosh
> Horizon International Ministries

"We've been introduced to Jesus, but *now* we've been introduced to the Father in a way we never have been before! I can't tell you how knowing that you are loved by the Father sets you up for life abundant instead of death. It has brought rest to my soul and helped release me to better respond to God's working in my life."

Nancy

"The My Dad Loves Me series has brought me freedom and a sense of cleanliness. These two words have new meaning for me. Having grown up in an abusive home, I have once again learned to 'feel' emotions I had long ago shut down. (Going back and reflecting on the love of God revealed to me during this series still causes me to cry months later). For the first time in my life, I truly feel that I belong to a family!"

Darla

"I have been a Christian for twenty years and have had a meaningful and loving relationship with my Heavenly Father during most of that time. What this series did for me, though, was to reveal twisted ways of thinking that I had carried over from my childhood to my relationship with the Lord. I was forced to take a new look at some things I had learned, to "invalidate" them, and let the truth of who God was really sink into my heart. It was painful at times, but worth it. For the first time in my life, I can begin to believe that God really *wants* to provide all my needs, and I have a new sense of assurance that God loves me—even when I blow it. Strongholds have been torn down—thoughts have been brought captive!"

Sandi

"The study on My Dad Loves Me made God's love for me real—not just a lofty principle but something I could take ownership of. It identified for me 'how' he loves me. Because I did not have a dad active in my life as I grew up, it personalized for me all the specific ways my Heavenly Father does show His love for me, and how this activity is worked out in my life. It also gave the whole subject of grace new meaning. This study pulled many things together for me."

Kathy

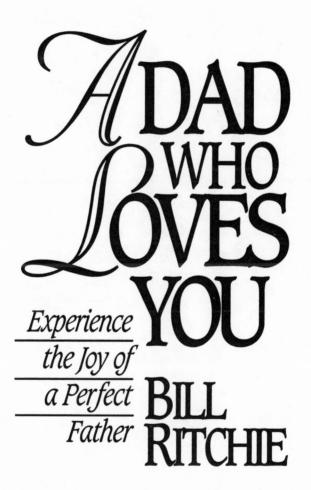

A DAD WHO LOVES YOU

Experience the Joy of a Perfect Father

BILL RITCHIE

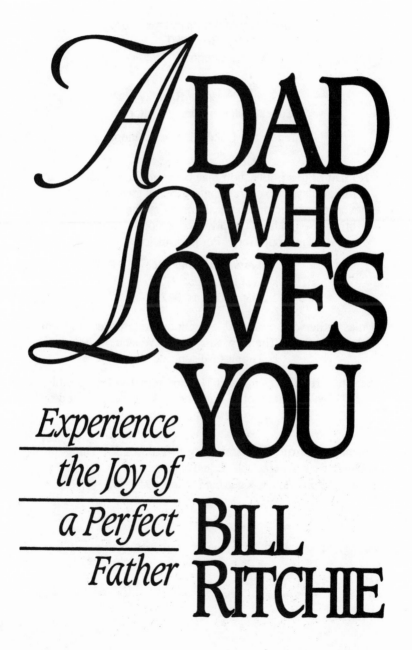

A DAD WHO LOVES YOU

Experience the Joy of a Perfect Father

BILL RITCHIE

A DAD WHO LOVES YOU
©1992 by Bill Ritchie

Published by Multnomah Press Books
P.O. Box 1720
Sisters, Oregon 97759

Edited by Steve Halliday
Cover design by Bruce DeRoos

Printed in the United States of America.

Questar Publishers, Inc.
Post Office Box 1720
Sisters, Oregon 97759

Unless otherwise indicated, all Scripture references are from
the Holy Bible: The New King James Version, © 1984 by
Thomas Nelson, Inc.

Scripture references marked TLB are from The Living Bible,
© 1971 by Tyndale House Publishers, Wheaton, Ill. Used by
permission.

Library of Congress Cataloging-in-Publication Data
(CIP information unavailable at time of printing.)
Library of Congress Catalogue Card Number 92-18466.

92 93 94 95 96 97 98 99 00 01 - 10 9 8 7 6 5 4 3 2

ACKNOWLEDGMENTS

Books are funny things; they don't seem terribly complex until you actually write one! If the Lord had not prompted me to write in the first place, I never would have begun the process. Had He not ministered His love and grace and strength along the way, I never would have persevered. Truly, to God be the glory!

From a human standpoint, my family was indispensable to the completion of this project. My wife, Betty, was really my first editor. She is my best friend and most ardent supporter. She's the greatest! If you don't think a Proverbs 31 wife exists, let me introduce you to her! My son Jason and his wife Alexa, my twins Geoffrey and Lisa, have always been in my corner. I owe to them far more than they will ever know. They allowed me to practice my "dad" skills, even through times of failure. You can't find better kids!

Finally, a word about my folks. More than anything else, my mom and dad believed in my brother, Doug, and me. More than that, if we were committed to it, whatever "it" was, they were with us one hundred percent. They were sure that somehow we would be able to pull "it" off! With a home environment like that, how could you not be willing to take a shot at the title?

Because my dad, Art, provided such a rock-solid base of stability for me, it is to him I dedicate this book. Though he went home to be with the Lord about two years ago, the foundation of security he established for me is something for which I shall be forever grateful.

A Dad Questionnaire

Before you begin reading this book, please take a couple of minutes to work through this questionnaire. Simply reading these questions will help you focus your thoughts on some important aspects of "dadhood" and on God as our heavenly Father. You'll benefit even more by writing out answers to the questions. You may be surprised at some our your responses!

1. What comes to mind when you hear the word "dad"?

2. What kind of relationship did you have with your dad when you were growing up?

3. What comes to mind when you hear that God is your father?

4. Is your relationship with God as father affected by your relationship with your own dad? If so, how?

5. (For parents) How has your relationship with your dad and your understanding of God as father affected the way you relate to your children?

Contents

CHAPTER ONE

A Dad Who Loves You

One of the most important people you will ever know, for better or for worse, is your dad.

Forget for a moment about what kind of relationship you had with your dad. The fact is, the man who biologically helped give you life or the man who had the most influence on your upbringing has an almost overpowering influence on everything you are and do.

Kendra's story captures the impact of "dad" far better than any psychological theories I might present. I'll tell you the rest of her story later, but for now let me give you a sketch of her childhood.

When Kendra was born, her mom was thirteen and her dad was seventeen—children rearing children. In no time at all, Kendra was joined by a sister. So now the young couple had two children to deal with.

On the surface, they were fundamental Christians. They belonged to a Bible church and were plugged into its many programs. Their faith was strong and real and deep. Or so it seemed.

Beneath the surface, things were quite different. Under the cover of night, in the quiet of her own home, Kendra's dad began to molest her sexually. She was just two years old. Over the next several years he abused her so often that she was forced to undergo colon reconstruction surgery while still a young girl.

Imagine the scars this treatment forced her to carry through her growing up years. Imagine the memories and messages she had to deal with. It seemed as though nothing made sense. Her immersion into a religiously fundamental environment prompted her to develop a thirst to know God. Yet did she really want a relationship with a God who would allow her to go through the kind of torture she had to endure? Could she ever trust someone who didn't seem to be there for her when she really needed Him? As she thought it through, she wondered: *Would God even want a relationship with me? Just look at how dirty and disgusting and repulsive I am. Certainly I deserved everything I got when I was growing up. I'm filthy inside. Why would a pure and powerful God desire to have me as His daughter?*

No matter how hard she tried, she couldn't shake the conflict. At age twenty-five while she was still struggling with whether God could love someone as "vile" as her, she expressed her feelings in the following poem:

As I walked upon the windy Oregon coast
I was enchanted by its unusual beauty;

the cliffs of green pine behind me,
white foam of rippling waves before me
and the fluffy clouds above.

The rustic, large driftwood
scattered along the beach
gave it an old age look;
I knew God was there.

As the sun shined upon my face
I prayed that God would show me the way
and I believed He would.

As I experienced the birds, jellyfish
and coarse sand beneath my feet
the wind kept blowing, forever changing
the waves, sand and clouds.

As I watched I wondered if God
had a plan for my life
and I hoped He did.
I now await for Him to reveal Himself;
after such a long time
I hope He hasn't
forgotten me.

God doesn't forget His children
so they say.
I only hope there is still room in His heart
for me.

Now, you tell me—does a dad make an impact
on his kids?

My own observation tells me that your dad affected
your life in one of two ways. He either worked to build
you up, or he worked to tear you down. His involvement wasn't simply neutral. It did *something*.

This was powerfully brought home to me recently

when I asked the people of my congregation to tell me about their dads. I put together a simple, non-scientific questionnaire designed to inquire about the impact a dad had on his kids. More than that, I wanted to understand how this relationship affected the way they related to God. I asked things like, "What comes to mind when you hear the word 'dad'?" "What kind of relationship did you have with your dad when you were growing up?"

People responded however they saw fit. There were only five questions, so they could reply with only five words if they so chose.

I was stunned by the response. Words cannot express the avalanche of emotion that my little survey generated. Within a few days I had received hundreds of replies. And while a few wrote only a couple of words, the vast majority poured out their souls. Some folks had such deep feelings that they sent back eight pages of material, typed and single-spaced!

I was shocked. I was completely unprepared for the ferocity of the reactions. People told me things they had never whispered to anyone. Ever. And while I gave them the opportunity to remain anonymous, less than a dozen questionnaires came in unsigned. They had things to say, they wanted to say them, and they wanted someone to know who was saying them. More than once I found written: "I have never told anybody about this before. You have no idea how much this means to me to get this off my chest, to bear the hurts of my heart with someone!"

As I read those responses over the next few days, it seemed I was always in tears—sometimes for joy, but much more often out of horror. While some folks had been marvelously affirmed by their dads, others had been devastatingly abused. If I didn't understand it before, it was now driven home to me in an unforgettable way: *Your dad has one of the greatest effects on you of anyone you will ever meet.* Anyone! Ever!

Indeed, I came to realize that our relationship with our dads continues to have a major impact on us whether they are alive or dead, close or indifferent, no matter if their influence was good, bad, or something else.

About 37.5 percent of the people reported they had terrific relationships with their dads. One of them wrote, "My dad loved me and always spoke well of me. He inspired me." Another said, "It was marvelous. My dad is responsible for everything I am today. He made me want to be a respectable, caring person, capable of being true to my word, having integrity, and knowing within myself that I can do whatever I choose to do and do it well. He was my prime example." A third reported, "My dad showed me how a man was supposed to behave as a husband and a father. He modeled character qualities such as honesty, responsibility, perseverance, hard work, mercy, and compassion." One woman told me, "I was Daddy's girl. My father brought me joy. Earliest memories of Dad were crawling up in his lap for a cuddle, an attentive ear to my great ventures, triumphs, and tragedies. He made me feel so good. To this day he attentively listens to my thoughts and to everyone else's viewpoints and troubles. He never pushes himself or accepts credit. Dad models what I need to practice but always fall short of—a humble spirit."

Wow! Isn't that great? Three-eighths of the hundreds who responded to the questionnaire said they had a good relationship with their dad. Their dad set for them a positive pace for the rest of their lives.

But if you're good at math you know the other shoe is about to drop. Not everyone had a glowing experience. Another 37.5 percent said they had a bad relationship with their dads. "My father was a violent, alcoholic, wife-beating child molester who took from his daughter what he couldn't get from his wife," wrote one woman. Another described her relationship with her dad like this: "It was stormy, full of hate, rejection, embarrassment, shame, confusion—secretive." "He was the warden and I was the prisoner," said another. One woman admitted her dad was "untrustworthy and engaged in verbal, physical, and emotional abuse. I was always fearful of him. I have never been good enough or done anything good enough to earn his praise." Still another wrote, "I hated and feared him. We never talked and when we did it was my dad yelling and screaming at me for something I did wrong. I was very stupid in his eyes." "My father was an alcoholic," said one respondent. "He beat my mother regularly. He sexually abused my sister and me, though my memories of this are limited. My images of him include that of a pitiful, slobbering, drunk. When I think of him, I think in terms of a big void."

It's a lot more fun reading about the first group, isn't it?

Last is the 25 percent who described their relationship with their dad as "indifferent." But if you read between the lines, you find it wasn't really so indifferent. One person wrote, "I had no relationship with my dad. He was gone most of my life and when he was home, he wasn't interested in me. He had no idea of what was going on in my head and my heart." Another reported, "He worked most of the time. We didn't know each other." "My dad kept me pretty much at arm's length for most of his life," wrote another. "His father did the same with him. I went to my mother for virtually everything." A fourth person said, "He was distant, not very emotionally involved. He provided for us but didn't take much time for play. He never really hugged me or said, 'I love you, Son.'" Yet another said, "He was not active with the children in my household at all. He just went to work, came home, and kept to himself." And finally, consider this comment: "Our relationship was distant, almost non-existent. I was always seeking his approval and affection but never seemed to get it. I always defended his actions, but inside I was hurt because he didn't ever give me the attention I desperately desired."

The fact that so rocked me on my heels was that fully five-eighths of those who responded to the questionnaire admitted they had a bad relationship with their dad. If I ever thought a dad wasn't a significant person in the lives of his kids, I had another think coming.

Psychiatrists use the term *parataxic distortion* to describe what often takes place in relationships. Parataxic distortion is defined as "any attitude toward another person which is based on a fantasied or distorted evaluation of that person or on an identification of that person with other figures from past experiences." Further, it is "a phenomenon in which feelings, thoughts, or expectations originating in one relationship are reenacted in another relationship, serving to distort the character of that latter relationship, and thus being inappropriate and anachronistic when applied."[1]

What does this mean in the context of "dad"? Just

this: if you had a bad relationship with your dad, you may very well have a distorted view of dads in general. And if you have a distorted view of dads in general, most of your relationships will be negatively affected. It doesn't make any difference whether you are male or female. It doesn't matter how old you are. It doesn't matter what kind of income you enjoy. Your flawed relationship with your dad will affect your relationship with authority figures. It will affect your relationship with men in general. It will affect your marriage. It will affect the way you relate to your kids. It will affect everything. A distorted image of dad will make it hard for you to see reality as it is.

But most important of all, a distorted view of dad will affect your view of God.

After all, isn't He supposed to be a dad? Isn't He sometimes called "the heavenly Father"? Judging both from the responses I got from the questionnaire and the reactions I encounter in counseling sessions, there is no question that a direct correlation exists between the relationship you had with your dad and your relationship to God as your Father. How could it be otherwise?

If your understanding of dad is negative, if you believe a dad is distant, uninterested in you, unavailable for you emotionally, how do you think that will play out in your relationship with God? It's going to be tremendously difficult for you to understand who God *really* is as your heavenly Father, your perfect Dad, because of the distorted images you pack around. Further, as long as you function with this distortion, you will find it almost impossible to be as happy or as healthy or as whole as you were designed to be.

But how do you go back and change what was?

How do you heal wounds that have scabbed over but are still very painful? How do you open up a future that until now has seemed nothing more than a wish, a hope, a dream?

In order for you to become healthy, to become all that you were created to be, the only answer is that you must digest certain key truths. You need to hear the facts. You need to soak for awhile in the healing balm of God's Word. That's what this book is designed to do.

In the Bible, God tells us what a perfect Dad is really like. Millions have found His Word to be true. He has never reneged on a promise. And one of the best of those promises is that, as your Dad, He will accept you unconditionally. He will forgive you all your faults. He will refuse to keep track of your failures.

Does that sound like a fairy tale? It's not. As we travel through this book together, your job is to allow these truths to wash over your mind and heart. Become marinated in their reality. It's true! And you can come to the place where you not only accept it as reality, but actually flow in it day by day.

The truth is, your heavenly Dad loves you with a love that defies understanding. He specializes in expressing His love for you in concrete ways.

Have you ever noticed that many religions seem to be nothing more than a bunch of concepts put down on paper? They're interesting to banter around philosophically, but there's no reality to them. Your heavenly Dad takes pains not to do that. He makes His truth tangible—no abstraction to it.

A long time ago a man named Thomas simply couldn't believe that Jesus had been raised from the dead. He hadn't yet seen the resurrected Lord, and even though several of his good buddies had seen Him, he just couldn't believe. Finally he said to his friends, "Listen. Unless I personally lay eyes on Him and unless I personally see in His hands the prints of the nails and put my finger into those prints and put my hand into his side, I'm not going to believe."

Shortly after his little speech he and several of his friends were together in a locked room. Jesus suddenly appeared in their midst. Without talking to anyone else in the room, He looked at Thomas and said, "Thomas my man, go for it. Come over here. I want you to reach your finger here and look at my hands. Reach your hand here and put it into my side. Don't be unbelieving, but believe." Jesus made tangible what for Thomas had been nothing more than an abstraction.

If you want to know how your heavenly Dad operates, just look at Jesus. Watch the way He operates. Understand how He functions. He doesn't want you merely to know about His love; He wants to show it to you. Straight up, so there is no mistaking what it is all about and how it is to take shape in your life.

This book is built upon two foundational truths:

1. If you want a perfect Dad, you can have one in the person of God the Father.

2. If you want to know what that perfect Dad is like, observe His Son, Jesus Christ.

"But Bill, it's not that easy," you say. "You don't understand. I had an awful dad, an ogre of a man. He abused me in ways I can't even describe. I'd love to think that God is different—but how can I? I can't 'just believe.' I hate my life and my situation, but what can I do? I don't know how to change it."

My friend, if that's your situation, I think I can help. It is possible for you to enjoy life with God as your Dad. You can begin to experience His joy and His peace—but there are several steps you need to take.

First, if you want a relationship with God as your Dad, you must earnestly desire it. You have to hunger for it. God is not going to force Himself on you. He is not going to inflict His will on you. You may have a dad who inflicted much more than his will on you. He may have inflicted his desires on you, he may have hurt you, he may have shattered your life in your tender, early years. But your heavenly Dad doesn't operate that way. The only way you are going to enter into a relationship with Him is by desiring it. You must want His love. He promises He will be there for you if you want Him to be. But you're the one who initiates the relationship.

Second, you must be willing to walk through some pain if you are to enjoy the gain found only in a relationship with God. Why? Because as you begin to understand what a dad really is, images of your own painful past and struggles and heartache will begin to surface.

I know you may not want to deal with that. You're no different than those who wrote to me, "I don't want to think about this. I don't want to remember these things. I don't want anything to do with them." When I first taught this material to my own congregation, one man in the audience sobbed through the entire first message—and the second, and the third. But finally he began to come to grips with his own painful past and he moved beyond it to a joyful new relationship with his heavenly Dad.

The problem is, you function in relationship to your past whether you want to or not. Past events can hold you captive. God wants to break their hold on you—but the only way to do that is by being willing to move through that pain so God can set you free once and for all.

Maybe it's easier to understand this example. Imagine that you broke your leg and then it was badly set or wasn't set at all. As a consequence, your leg doesn't work right—it doesn't enjoy full mobility or do what it's supposed to do. Therefore you're wobbling through life like a cork on unsteady seas. Now you have two choices: either you can go through the rest of your life that way and watch things get worse and worse and perhaps see your leg freeze up altogether, or you can have it rebroken and reset that it might grow correctly, thereby giving you full mobility. It's your choice. You can live the rest of your life crippled, or you can live the rest of your life set free.

It's true this process does not feel good. Who wants to have his leg broken unnecessarily? Not me. But the truth is, unless you're willing to face that pain, you're never going to be healthy. Unless you're willing to go through the hurt of being set free from the bondage of the past, you're never going to walk in the wholeness God desires for you.

And don't forget—you're not going to walk through any of this alone! When you enter into a relationship with your heavenly Dad, He's there with you. He's ministering His life and His love and His health to you all the way through . . . but you have to be willing to go through the pain. To be honest, that may be the toughest part of the process.

The third critical step—and it's where I want to camp in this book—calls for you to be immersed, soaked in God's truth. His Word, the Bible, is truth with a capital T. It is reality with a capital R. Whatever you may or may not have experienced is a distant shadow of truth. The Bible is God's truth. He is the perfect Dad. If you want to understand who a dad is and how a dad operates, all you need to do is to immerse yourself in His reality. Allow your mind to be reprogrammed so that, for the first time in your life, you can have a true image of a dad. A Dad who will always be there for you. A Dad who will always minister to you.

Fourth, you must be willing to let your heavenly Dad put your past to rest. Only in that way will your future open up. You'll never be able to see the sunrise if you spend all your time looking at the sunset. You'll never be able to turn around and be set free if you spend your life focused on all your wounds and hurts and struggles and pain. You can't race into the life that God has for you by running backward.

Frankly, it doesn't matter if you are ten years old or eighty. It doesn't matter what you may have lost. It doesn't matter what you may not have experienced. God is saying to you today, "This day I want to be your Dad, and this day everything you have ever wanted—and so much more!—is yours. Here, it's yours. Take it." But you have to be willing to extend your hand.

God Himself is the Dad you've always wanted. He is a perfect Dad who loves you and wants to give you life. All He asks is that you trust Him in order to have that life.

You may never have experienced the love of a

human dad, but your heavenly Dad longs to take you in His almighty arms right now, right where you are, right this very minute.

If you've already begun this marvelous relationship with God as your heavenly Dad, prepare yourself to learn more about what He's really like and what He wants to accomplish in your life. You can have a Dad who loves you! In the following pages, let's learn together just how far-reaching His love is.

Note
1. Daniel J. Heinrichs, "Our Father Which Art in Heaven: Parataxic Distortions in the Image of God," *Journal of Psychology and Theology*, Summer 1982, 10(2), 121-122.

My Dad Accepts Me

How would you describe the perfect dad?

Since the television media is so dominant in creating values and concepts in our culture, my guess is that TV has helped mold your description of the perfect dad. Depending on how old you are, that description would take a slightly different shape.

If you're over forty, you probably imagine some combination of the best qualities of the dads on "Father Knows Best," "The Adventures of Ozzie and Harriet," and "Leave It to Beaver." Jim, Ozzie, and Ward definitely had their positive points!

If you're a bit younger, you might feel more at home with Charles Ingalls on "Little House on the Prairie." And if you relate to none of the above, how about Cliff Huxtable of "The Cosby Show"?

When you get right down to it, all these dads have several things in common. When you move beyond the different styles of dress, jokes, and asides, all of them seem to possess the same positive characteristics. They are strong, loving, secure, and patient. They seem to be understanding beyond measure and unbelievably accepting. That's the quality that really stands out—their acceptance.

Ricky Nelson used to do some crazy things, but Ozzie always accepted him. Kathy, the little girl on "Father Knows Best," continually got herself into little girl scrapes—but Jim was always there, accepting and loving her just the way she was. And what about Dr. Huxtable? Sondra, Denise, Theo, Vanessa, and Rudy have a dad who always accepts them—with or without earrings! No matter what they've done or what kind of trouble they cause, Cliff always hangs in there for them.

That's the nice thing about TV dads. Whatever your situation in life, for at least half an hour each week you can turn on that show, crawl into your TV set, forget about "real life," and, for a while at least, vicariously live with a model family. For one tiny moment, their dad is yours. You feel what it's like to be loved and accepted for who you are. You're forgiven, set free to grow up the way you were meant to. Terrific!

Sadly, TV dads live only one place: TV. Most of us didn't have dads quite like that. My mail indicates that it's the overwhelming minority who had good dads.

What if you're one of the unfortunates who didn't have a prime-time kind of dad? What if your dad wasn't accepting and forgiving? What if you didn't have a dad who was there to praise and affirm you? How do you fill in the gap for what never was? How do you create warm feelings out of thin air?

Though the following situations may seem extreme, let me tell you the stories of three of my friends. I think you'll get a better understanding of where many people come from.

Rita's Story

Rita lived her early life under intense pressure to perform. Her dad was a professional, extremely adept at what he did. He expected his kids to be just as good as he was . . . in everything.

He signed them up for lessons every night of the week. Each one took instruction in something on Monday, Tuesday, Wednesday, Thursday, and Friday nights. Ah, but Saturday was different; Saturday's lesson lasted all day.

They'd move from tap to ballet to piano to violin to art—you name it, they did it. And through it all, their dad expected them not only to excel, but to become the very best in everything they tried.

Today, Rita cannot remember a single time in her entire childhood when her dad said, "You did a good job." All she can remember is him screaming at her to do better. She recalls his reddened face, veins bulging at the neck, yelling at her to work harder to accomplish what he expected her to do. But a compliment? A word of encouragement? An expression of affection? Forget it.

Rita desperately wanted to live up to her dad's expectations. She longed to be accepted. She craved a simple hug. But she couldn't and she wasn't and she never got one. No matter what she did, it was never good enough.

To this day Rita finds herself not only struggling with bitterness, but saddled with timidity and a total unwillingness to risk. She's scared to death that she might foul up. If she did, who would accept her? Even her own dad wouldn't.

Sue's Story

And then there's Sue. Sue did live in the Huxtable household, or so everyone thought. Outsiders envied her all-American family. They were good looking and appeared to be on top of everything.

Especially her dad. Some men need to be poked with a cattle prod before they'll set foot in church. Not her dad. Church was his life. He was completely invested there. He sat on the board, he sang in the choir, he taught Sunday school. He did everything there was to do. So did his wife and kids.

Sue's family was the picture of perfection, the type of family that others would point to and hope that somehow they could emulate. A wonderful, ideal, all-American family.

Or so it seemed.

Once they got home and shut the doors, the picture changed. Radically. It was classic "Dr. Jekyll and Mr. Hyde." Sue's dad could have written the part. While the outside world respected him as Dr. Jekyll, he was Mr. Hyde at home.

Sue could never do anything well enough for her dad. He always pressured her to be right, to do right, to act right, to look right. But no matter what she was, no matter what she did, no matter how she acted, it was never quite good enough.

That's when the belittling words came rocketing toward her like angry missiles. That's when the haranguing would start and never let up. Even as a little child Sue was made to feel like a piece of garbage (her words). Absolutely worthless.

As a young girl trying to fulfill levels of expectation that were beyond her reach, she made a decision most parents would love for their children to make. She decided she was never going to rebel. And she didn't.

It wasn't out of love, however, that she made that decision. It was out of fear. She made it because she didn't want to incur the wrath of her dad.

From then on she did everything just the way she was supposed to. She got straight A's. She became the best musician in the area. She rose to the top of everything she tried. She became an achiever, even an overachiever.

Still it wasn't good enough. Her dad was not impressed. Never did she hear him say, "You're really okay just the way you are."

She vividly remembers coming home one night after a date with a high school guy whom her dad greatly admired. They returned one minute late. Sixty ticks of the clock. Not bad for a pair of high schoolers, right?

Her dad didn't see it that way. He grounded her for two weeks. "How in the world could you violate my standards?" he stormed. What a filthy piece of trash his little girl was—to tarnish a perfect childhood by daring to come home from a date sixty seconds late.

Linda's Story

Last, meet Linda. Linda grew up in a household similar to Sue's, except in Linda's case the standard of perfection kept shifting. She was forced to aim at a moving target without ever knowing in which direction the target was headed.

Once her dad challenged her to get an A in a class that was hard for her. She accepted the challenge and poured herself into that class. She gave it every extra minute she had, every ounce of energy she could muster. And she made it. She got an A.

Beaming with pride, she walked into the living room and handed her report card to her dad. He looked at it and snorted, "Why didn't you get all A's? What's your problem? Didn't you work hard enough?"

No matter what she did, it simply wasn't good enough.

Linda found herself constantly trying to please her dad . . . and constantly failing. When she was eleven years old he slipped up and paid her a compliment. "You know, your face is becoming kind of cute," he whispered to her. Linda was so stunned by the comment that she ran into her bedroom, grabbed a tape recorder, ran back into the kitchen, plugged it in, and asked him to repeat what she had just heard. She wanted to have it on record to play it over and over again to herself. At eleven years old, she knew she would never again hear her dad say anything remotely resembling such a remark. And she was right. She didn't.

Linda's dad didn't limit his standards of perfection to his daughter alone. He passed them around to the whole family. His son was gifted intellectually, a tremendous athlete, and possessed all kinds of other natural abilities that most people would kill for. But he was never good enough for his dad.

As a consequence, he went through life always

struggling to be something he could never be. He became an alcoholic. He entered and left five marriages. Throughout his life he kept striving for a constantly changing goal, a goal just out of reach.

He was especially good at sales. He worked for a large, national company and became one of its best salesmen. In fact, he was so good that for thirty-four months in a row he topped the national sales charts. Finally, at a sales convention attended by the entire nationwide sales force, Linda's brother was recognized for his achievement. He was asked to come forward to receive an award for his unprecedented success.

As they handed him the award, he turned and looked at the national sales manager. With tears in his eyes he whispered, "I'll do better next year, really I will."

All of his dad's old tapes were still playing, blaring out their poisonous message loudly and insistently in his heart. He still felt he wasn't good enough. The trophy was nice and so was the recognition, but what he really needed was a word of acceptance . . . from his dad. He was desperate for it.

It's possible you grew up in a real "Father Knows Best" family, that you were accepted, forgiven, praised, and encouraged along the way. But I doubt it. If you're like most of the people I meet and minister to, it's not Cliff Huxtable who comes to mind when you think of your dad.

If you're like most people in this society, you wonder how in the world you'll ever fill that ache in your life, that void caused by an uncaring or absent dad. You wonder how to get past that feeling, that hunger, that desire, just to know that you're okay the way you are.

What They Saw Is What You Get

There is a Dad who can give you all that, and more. God offers to anyone who wants it the opportunity to become His son, His daughter. Through faith in His Son, Jesus Christ, He offers to give you—whether you're fifteen years old or ninety-five years old—everything that a perfect Dad should be able to give you. That's infinitely more than Cliff Huxtable or Jim Anderson or Ward Cleaver ever thought to offer.

All it takes to receive such an offer is a willingness to enter into a relationship with God as your Dad through Jesus Christ. Do that, and you can obtain, right now, what you've never dared imagine could be yours.

I suspect, however, that you're skeptical. You've never seen such a dad (except on TV) and you doubt one could really exist. If you feel that way, I invite you to come with me on a tour. One of the best ways to see how our Dad accepts us unconditionally is to look at the life of Jesus. Jesus himself said, "He who has seen Me has seen the Father" (John 14:9). If you want to know how God treats His kids, watch Jesus. If you see Jesus unconditionally loving His kids, you know that's the way God does it, too. It's staggering to see Him at work.

Let's visit just a few of the scenes where Jesus shows us the full meaning of unconditional love. There are so many such instances it's almost impossible to count them. But let me recall just a few.

As you join me on this trip back to ancient Palestine, remind yourself it is not just words on a page but the absolute truth. There really is a perfect Dad for anyone who will receive Him!

The Moral Zero

Let's start by considering a woman whose life was one big moral failure. Her story is told in chapter 8 of the book of John.

The tale begins with this unnamed woman getting caught in the act of adultery. There was no question about it; she was found naked in bed with a married man. According to Jewish law, she should have been stoned to death.

The Pharisees and the scribes dragged her to Jesus, threw her at His feet, and asked Him what should be done. They knew He didn't have any choice—the law was the law. He had no option but to pronounce judgment on her and consent to her stoning.

But Jesus had a few surprises up His cloak. John tells us that Jesus hesitated, wrote something in the sand, then looked each man in the eye and said, "He who is without sin among you, let him be the first to throw a stone at her." He invited them to hum some rocks at her. "Go for it! Any one of you standing here whose life is perfect, give her your best shot."

Nobody did. One by one, without so much as picking up a pebble, they walked away. Jesus then looked at the woman and said to her, "Where are your accusers? Hasn't anybody condemned you?"

She looked around nervously and said, "No."

"I don't condemn you either," replied Jesus. "Go and sin no more."

Don't forget the particulars of this story. This woman is guilty. Caught in the act. She's worthy of death. But Jesus reaches out and accepts her, unconditionally. Wow!

The White-collar Robber Baron

We see Jesus doing the same thing in Luke 19 with a known extortionist. Zacchaeus was a Jew who worked as a chief tax collector for the Romans. To be a tax collector was bad enough. In those days, the only way you could get such a job was through graft, corruption, and extortion. But to become a chief tax collector, a supervisor, you had to elevate your game to a whole new level of graft and corruption and extortion. That's what Zacchaeus did. That's who he was.

Luke tells us that as Jesus was traveling through the town of Jericho, Zacchaeus shimmied up a tree to have a look at him. That was the best way for a short guy like Zacchaeus to get a good glimpse—people were crowding around Jesus and it was hard to get near Him. As Jesus walked past Zacchaeus's perch, He stopped dead in his tracks, looked up, and said, "Zach, I'd like to come over and have lunch with you today. Would that work for you?"

The religious people were aghast. How could Jesus do such a thing? Didn't He know what kind of man Zacchaeus was?

But it didn't bother Jesus at all. He honestly wanted to spend some time with this man. So He went over to Zach's house and said to him, "Salvation has come to your house today." He accepted Zacchaeus just the way he was.

The Social Outcast

If that doesn't do it for you, how about this one? It's found in the eighth chapter of Luke. Jesus once accepted a woman who was ceremonially impure because of a physical ailment. This woman had been bleeding for twelve years. She tried everything and hired countless doctors, but nobody was able to help her. None of the Jews would go near her. She well knew what it was to be excluded from polite company. Her social life was zip.

But did her problem bother Jesus? No way. He accepted her just the way she was, and healed her just as He met her. He didn't tell her, "Lady, if you'll just get your life together and get healthy, then we'll talk." No. Instead, He met her where she was, just as she was. That's acceptance.

The Public Health Hazard

Still not convinced? Then meet a man who suffered from a horrible disease, even worse than AIDS is considered in this culture. The man had leprosy.

Leprosy was so vile and struck such fear in the people that the mere appearance of a leper was enough to send people screaming away in terror. Lepers were required to hang a cloth over their faces and yell out, "Unclean, unclean," as they walked onto any street. That way the healthy people could flee without taking the chance of breathing the air that moments before filled the lepers' lungs.

Wouldn't it have made sense for Jesus to be uptight about such a man, too? Not a chance. The first chapter of Mark tells us that Jesus, moved with compassion, put out His hand and touched the leper, sores and all. Touched him! Not only did He dare to breathe the same air, not only did He accept the man, but He touched him. No one did that! And with one touch, Jesus gave the man's life back to him. He healed him on the spot.

If you don't think that man felt accepted, we must not be talking about the same incident.

The Tramp, the Blind Man, and the Thief

A woman described in chapter 4 of the book of John had a very checkered history. She'd married five guys and was living with a sixth. Jesus initiated a conversation with her and instead of condemning her immorality, accepted her and offered her the same "Dad deal" I'm telling you about right now. She accepted.

The eighteenth chapter of Luke tells of a blind man, a total outcast. Sitting by a roadside with a crowd milling around him, he heard Jesus was passing by. That was enough for him. At the top of his lungs he shouted, "Jesus, Son of David, have mercy on me!" The crowd turned to him and screamed, "Shut up! You're always such a bother. You always get in the way. You are an embarrassment to us. Just be quiet! Let this guy go by. We want to cheer and applaud Him. We don't want to listen to you!"

Their threats didn't faze this poor man. He kept yelling until Jesus heard his cries, stopped, made His way through the crowd, and healed him. Remember, this was a reject, an outcast, a throwaway. At least, that's what the crowd thought of him. It isn't what he was to Jesus. At that moment in time, he was the most important person in the world.

Or consider one last incident that occurred at the very end of Jesus' life. If ever there were a time Jesus could forget about other people, wouldn't it be at His own crucifixion? Talk about problems. At that instant, He had more problems than we'll ever know. But Jesus isn't like that.

As He was hanging on the cross, dying, He looked at a convicted thief hanging next to Him and said, "Today, you will be with Me in paradise." How could that be? The man didn't have time to atone for his sin. He couldn't return to all the people he'd robbed and make it right with them. Yet none of that seemed to get in Jesus' way. He accepted that thief right where he was, just as he was—just as He did with the very ones who nailed Him to the cross. Looking at the men who wrongfully crucified Him, He said, "Father, forgive them. They don't know what they are doing."

That's Our Dad!

We've looked only at the tip of the iceberg. Time and again Jesus accepted people unconditionally. He forgave them of their faults. He refused to keep track of their shortcomings and never threw their sins back in their faces.

That's precisely the picture you need to keep in mind of the Dad who wants a relationship with you as His child.

But before we go any further, I have to ask: Have you accepted His love through Jesus? Have you become His child—His son, His daughter? Have you trusted Him for eternal life? That's where it all begins.

If you don't know God as your heavenly Dad, ask Him to make you His son or His daughter right now. Believe that He raised His Son, Jesus Christ, from the dead. Demonstrate your faith in Him to wipe out all of your sins by placing your trust in Jesus as your Lord and Savior. Do it now.

Once you've done that, the sky's the limit.

John wrote about this in the first chapter of his Gospel. Speaking about Jesus, he wrote, "But as many as received Him, to them He gave the right to become children of God" (John 1:12). We have been invited to become God's sons, God's daughters—our heavenly Dad's kids. To everyone who receives Jesus, He gives the right to become God's kids. "Even to those who believe in His name: who were born not of blood, nor of the will of the flesh, nor of the will of man, but of God."

Or look at what Paul says in Galatians 4:4-7: "But when the fullness of the time had come, God sent forth His Son, born of a woman, born under the law, to redeem those who were under the law, that we might receive the adoption as sons [and daughters]. And because you are sons [and daughters], God has sent forth the Spirit of His Son into your hearts, crying out, 'Abba, Father!' [Dad!]. Therefore you are no longer a slave but a son [or a daughter], and if a son [or daughter], then an heir of God through Christ."

A Dad Who Will Love You

If you want it, you can have a relationship with the perfect Dad by believing in Jesus. And the only thing that can keep you out of that relationship is you. God isn't going to force Himself on you, but He does make Himself available to you. He wants to be your Dad. If you want one, you can have a perfect Dad, God the Father. He is there for you simply by your believing in Jesus Christ.

Jesus spent His whole life on earth trying to show us what His Father was like so that we would choose to become a member of His family. "He who has seen Me has seen the Father," Jesus said. If you want to know what unconditional acceptance feels like, if you want to experience how a perfect Dad operates, then listen to Jesus. When you ask His Father to become your Dad, you'll instantly know what it is to be accepted right where you are, just as you are. He doesn't ask you first to change so that you'll be okay. He doesn't tell you to stop anything, to get rid of anything, to become anything. He just tells you that if you desire His love He'd love to give it to you. Right now. Right where you are.

That's the perfect Dad who invites you to share in His life. For all those who take Him up on His offer, I have fantastic news: Because your Dad loves you, He accepts you unconditionally.

Getting It From the Head to the Heart

It's one thing to know all these things intellectually; it's quite another to get that truth to drift downward into your heart where it can change the way you live. My promise is this: if you can accept what the Bible says is true, you won't have to continue to fight the dark images from your past. I'd like to give you four suggestions that might help you to do this.

1. Acknowledge that God's Word isn't only for other people.

God's Word is for you, too. God's Word wasn't written for religious people alone. It wasn't written just for good people. It wasn't given solely to people who have their lives together. God's Word was written for you.

You may feel so worthless, so filled with shame and guilt that it's hard to believe that the God of creation could accept you. "He may have done that for other people," you say, "but that's them and I'm me; I know how bad my life really is."

There's an old song I used to sing years ago. I knew it even before I knew the Lord, because my

Grandma used to sing it. What a tremendous truth it declares:

> It is no secret what God can do.
> What He's done for others, He'll do for you.
> With arms wide open, He'll pardon you.
> It is no secret what God can do.

No, His Word wasn't written only for somebody else. It was written for you.

2. Recognize that your earthly dad and your perfect Dad are not the same person.

Your earthly dad and your perfect Dad are two very different people. Your earthly dad may have hurt you, he may have belittled you, he may have constantly chipped away at your self-worth. He may have let you down. He may have kept score of every failure in your life and known just exactly the right time to throw them back in your face. He may have done all of that—but that's not your perfect Dad. That is not the God of creation.

You must reaffirm that these are two very different people and that it is your perfect Dad who promises to accept you right where you are, just as you are.

3. If you need to do so, confess your faults to your perfect Dad, whether they are real or imagined.

In the end, it doesn't make any difference whether you feel dirty because of things you've done or because of how others have made you feel. You feel how you feel. That's where you've got to start.

The truth is, you may have blown it. There may be areas where you've made a big-time mess of things. So confess that to your perfect Dad. He's not going to rain heaven down upon you to crush you, to stamp you, to say, "See, I told you what a creep you are!" In fact, the Bible tells us that, "If we confess our sins, He is faithful and just to forgive us and cleanse us."

He wants you to feel clean. He wants you to be clean. He wants to set you free from the grip of shame, from the tentacles of remorse. But if you are ever going to get free, you will have to confess your sins and shortcomings to the Lord. Call them for what they are. Tell Him exactly how you are feeling. He wants that burden off your back—you don't need to carry it one minute longer.

4. Sear into your mind and speak with your lips the precious truths of how your perfect Dad loves and accepts you.

May I list a few of those truths for you? Listen closely as they are personalized for you:

"Come to Me, all you who labor and are heavy laden, and I will give you rest" (Matthew 11:28).

"Though your sins are like scarlet, they shall be as white as snow; Though they are red like crimson, they shall be as wool" (Isaiah 1:18).

"As far as the east is from the west, so far has He removed our transgressions [sins] from us" (Psalm 103:12).

"I am the bread of life. He who comes to Me shall never hunger, and he who believes in Me shall never thirst" (John 6:35).

"For I am persuaded that neither death nor life, nor angels nor principalities nor powers, nor things present nor things to come, nor height nor depth, nor any other created thing, shall be able to separate us from the love of God which is in Christ Jesus our Lord" (Romans 8:38-39).

Or that beautiful and powerful word that He speaks to us in Revelation 3:20: "Behold, I stand at the door and knock. If anyone hears My voice and opens the door, I will come in to him and dine with him, and he with Me."

That's typical of the things your perfect Dad wants for you. Because your Dad loves you, He accepts you unconditionally right where you are, just as you are. He promises to forgive you all your faults and He pledges not to keep track of your failures. Your perfect Dad loves you that much. That is the basis upon which He desires you to build a new life as His son, as His daughter. Hear Him speaking to you today: "Because I am your Dad, I love you with a love that will not quit. I accept you right where you are, just as you are, that you might have life in Me." The truth is, the news could not be better:

Because your Dad loves you, He accepts you unconditionally.

CHAPTER THREE

My Dad Guides Me

Dads are supposed to have wisdom—at least a reservoir, if not an ocean! They're also supposed to possess the ability and desire to dispense it to their children at precisely the right moment. Or so our folklore would suggest.

Fortunately, folklore isn't always wrong. Some people actually did grow up with dads who fit this description. They did have wisdom. They did have desire. And they consistently worked to guide their children through life.

"My dad provided encouragement and enabled me to recognize meaning, purpose, and direction for my life" Joan wrote to me. "He fostered me in my talents, my formal education, and my career choices. He made sure I would be able to survive in this world when I would finally move away on my own. Dad was my teacher. He taught me about God's love and demonstrated that love. He led me at the age of six to trust Jesus as my Savior during one of our regular family devotional times. Dad was my example for spiritual things as well as for earthly things, because he not only taught me God's Word, he taught me common sense, helped me understand the hows and whys of things and the circumstances of life, and encouraged me to think for myself. He taught me through just punishment—always explaining, always quoting God's principles and Word, always gentle even when angry. He expressed disapproval without belittlement. He earned my respect and honor because he did what was right in the sight of the Lord. Somehow, he always made me aware that God was in control of his life."

Some dads operate that way. If you had a dad like that, be grateful.

Dan didn't have such a dad, but he had the next best thing. He grew up in a single-parent home where his dad had to be gone a lot with his work. That meant Dan didn't receive the kind of guidance at key moments that he needed. Happily, however, Dan's granddad stepped in and filled that role. In fact, he and Dan's grandma moved to the area where Dan was living just so they could fill this key role.

When Dan was sixteen years old he decided to learn how to hunt. All his school friends were hunters and Dan thought it would be fun to join them. There was just one problem: who could teach him how to hunt? He wanted to join his friends, but he didn't want to appear ignorant in front of them.

So, grandpa to the rescue! He jumped right in when Dan told him what he wanted to do. He helped his grandson get a license, took him out to the woods, and taught him how to hunt. What a time they had! Call it beginner's luck, but Dan bagged a deer his first time out. It was a proud moment when they hauled it out of the truck and up to the house.

Dan's story may not seem so unusual, except for one thing: Dan's grandpa was blind. So when hunting lessons began, it was Dan who drove the car, Dan who carried the gun, and Dan who packed the pack. But once they got to the right spot, it was grandpa who talked Dan through everything he needed to know about hunting. Did it ever work!

Dan broke his back when he was nineteen and by the time hunting season rolled around, he was still recuperating. But he was so hooked on hunting that he couldn't imagine missing a season. Especially when there was game out there with his name on it! He just had to get out there some way. But how? Neither he nor his grandpa were able to do the things required in order to hunt. So Grandpa did the only thing he could.

He conscripted Grandma.

Hunting day dawned bright and early with grandma at the wheel. Grandma packed the gun and grandma led all three to the appropriate place. When all the details had been handled, Grandpa picked up right where he left off by guiding his grandson in another successful hunt.

Yes, there really are some dads and granddads out there who give great guidance to their kids. They seem to know what to do and enjoy guiding their offspring.

Unfortunately, there are a lot of dads who don't fit this mold at all. They produce a legion of kids who struggle for years trying to figure out exactly what to do with their lives. Nobody has shown any interest or taken the time to help them. So what are they supposed to do?

Tom knows what it's like to feel this way. He grew up in a single-parent family in which dad was never around. Underline "never." It was up to mom to rear Tom and his two brothers, and it was everything she could do to provide for her family, keep up the house, run after three kids, and occasionally go out on dates. By the time she was finished, she had no energy left. At least, that's how she felt. She wasn't able to provide Tom with any real guidance at the significant moments when he most needed it. And even though Tom's dad was very much alive, he had zero interest in doing anything to guide his son.

Throughout his school career, Tom percolated to the top. He was the class clown and extremely talented— one of those people who did well at anything he attempted. His sense of humor and his ability to move into situations and take control enabled him to get along well with everybody. All the way through school he was extremely popular.

At the end of his senior year, during the first part of May, Tom bounced into the guidance counselor's office to talk. He was excited to find out which of five or six colleges would give him the best scholarship to finance his educational future.

The guidance counselor looked at him in disbelief and said, "Tom, those scholarships were handed out months ago. Why didn't you come to see me earlier, like last fall? With your grades and the tardiness of the application, you wouldn't be able to get into any of these schools. If you had been interested in doing something like this, you should have been applying months ago. Where in the world have you been? What were you thinking? Tom, I'm sorry, but you'd better think about the local community college. There may still be a spot for you there."

Dazed and reeling from his dreadful discovery, Tom politely made his way out of the office. Once in the hall, even though he was a big, strapping guy, he broke down sobbing. Why hadn't anyone told him? Why didn't he get the guidance he needed when he needed it?

Now, you know as well as I do that Tom's school had made announcements all year to make sure graduating seniors were on track. Papers had been handed out concerning appropriate tests and dates, visitations of college recruiters had been announced, and care was taken to assure students of the best possible chance to get into the college of their choice.

That wasn't the problem. The problem was Tom was a seventeen-year-old boy who needed somebody to nudge him along to the next appropriate step—but he didn't have a dad at home who was making sure his son was taking care of business. He had no one to ensure that certain decisions were being made on time, applications were sent along with fees, tests were taken. The result: Tom was stuck.

Everybody Needs Guidance

You'd be amazed at how many times I have counseled with people just like Tom—people totally confused about what to do with their lives. They have no sense of direction. Nobody has ever walked them through the process of life. No one has helped them along the way to learn how to make decisions.

Some dads never took the time to guide their kids. Other dads didn't know how. Still other dads had never grown up themselves and so had nothing to guide their kids with.

The result? After years of struggling in life, unable to make even the most basic decisions about jobs and spouses and all the rest, they give up. They wander through life, aimless, directionless, joyless, often feeling angry or frustrated or incomplete because of something they desperately desired but never had.

If you are to grow up to be a person who is whole and mature and complete, you have to be guided somewhere along the line.

But what if no one has provided you with guidance? What do you do if there is no reservoir from which to draw, no foundation on which to build? Worse, what happens when you are counted on to give guidance that you yourself never had? What if you, like a lot of other people, never had a dad to guide you?

The Bible gives a comforting and helpful answer to such questions. It assures you that when you enter into a relationship with God as your Dad, He guides you. In fact, as you get to know Him, you find He has been actively guiding you even before He became your Dad. More than that, you discover He wants to make available to you all the resources it takes to build you up to be the kind of person you so desire to be.

How do you gain this guidance? How do you put it to work? The Bible gives several answers to this. But before looking at them, realize this—everything hangs on your having entered into a relationship with God as your Dad. It all starts there. I don't mean to camp on this, but it is so essential to all that follows. If you haven't yet put your faith in Jesus Christ and asked God to be your Dad, there's no way He can provide the personal guidance you need. But as soon as you do, He promises to guide you. He'll do this in two ways:

1. By personal involvement

2. By powerful resources

Each of these gives a better picture of the depth and breadth of your perfect Dad's guidance.

Your Perfect Dad Invests Himself in You

No one is as concerned about you or as involved in your life as is God. And even more amazingly, your perfect Dad is profoundly invested in you whether you know it or not!

It may well be that if your earthly dad gave you no guidance, you assume your heavenly Dad has no inclination to do so, either. Judy certainly struggles with this. She says: "My dad is a vague figure who once said, 'If anything happens to your mother, you kids are on the street.' And so it was." Jim wrestles with the same sorts of feelings. "I can only remember five or six times that Dad and I did anything together. I don't think he loved me. He never said so. He never hugged me and he left us to fend for ourselves when I was about nine years old. When my dad finally died, I didn't care."

Both Judy and Jim confess to wondering, *why should God be any different?* You may have the same question.

I'm glad to say the Bible makes it clear that unlike

many earthly fathers, God is heavily involved in guiding His kids. He often works on their behalf even before they know Him. That was certainly true for the apostle Paul.

Paul was one of the best-educated young men of his day. He was a quick study and had a bent toward education. He studied under Gamaliel, the greatest rabbi of his day.

As students went, Paul was one of Gamaliel's all-time best. He learned the history of Judaism, studied its faith, and knew its scriptures backward and forward. He could debate theological fine points with the best of them.

Over time, he became so zealous and protective of his faith that he attacked anything he saw as a threat. Thus, he became a persecutor of Christians. After all, weren't they trying to destroy the faith that was the center of his life? Why should they be allowed to extend that which should be extinguished?

One day while on a seek-and-destroy mission, Paul's world turned upside down. Suddenly he was confronted by none other than Jesus Christ Himself. While you might think Christ should have destroyed Paul, He rather insisted that He desired a relationship with him.

This meeting so overwhelmed Paul that he began a whole new life. He believed in Christ and became part of God's family. God became his Dad in a whole new way!

So what did Paul's new Dad do with His kid's strict Jewish background? Did He trash it? Ignore it? Cover it up? Hardly. He pressed all of Paul's upbringing into service for Him. Far from viewing his education as a loss, as preparation for nothing, God rather transformed it into something to be used powerfully for His kingdom. Paul's energy and understanding simply had to be redirected.

Paul had a phenomenal grasp of God's Word. He understood the Jewish faith inside and out and could relate to those who were a part of it. In some cases, he could offer understandings that they themselves did not have. And his zeal! God took the very thing that almost destroyed the Church and used it to put Paul into places where angels feared to tread.

No, God was not unaware of Paul's education. God did not stand off to the side and say, "That's too bad—all of this time and study for nothing! What a waste!" God rather made certain that if Paul was a student, he might as well be a *good* one. And the apostle's knowledge came to be used for tremendous good!

As God became Paul's Dad, He became heavily invested in his life. He took the background that was so critical to shaping Paul's early years and molded it to be used for new and far more helpful purposes.

In a much less dramatic way, God did a similar thing in my life. Since junior high it seemed like I always ended up leading groups, speaking before gatherings, large and small. I was the first student body president of a new junior high school. As such, I had the opportunity to take part in many of the assemblies. Later, as junior class president, I moderated weekly assemblies for more than two thousand students. Because we had so many students and an auditorium that held only about one thousand, that meant I had to do two assemblies each week.

I wasn't involved with the Lord at the time so the

thought that He was refining me for His service through the crucible of these assemblies never occurred to me. In fact, had I known God was preparing me for "multiple services" on Sunday mornings, I'm not sure I would have run for office at all.

How reassuring it is to know that God is personally involved in guiding His kids! He is so committed to guiding them that He is often doing so even when they don't know it. When God is your Dad, count on Him being personally involved in your life.

No Scarcity of Powerful Resources

Our perfect Dad also guides His kids by means of some powerful resources. It is no exaggeration to say that there is no resource that God withholds when it comes to guiding His kids.

One of the most obvious and yet most powerful of these resources is the Bible. Psalm 1:1-2 states as well as anything the way in which this resource guides those who use it:

> Blessed is the man
> who walks not in the counsel of the ungodly,
> nor stands in the path of sinners,
> nor sits in the seat of the scornful;
> but his delight is in the law of the LORD,
> and in His law he meditates day and night.

How can you become a happy person? The happiest person is the one who gets most excited about his or her Dad's guidance—the one who chooses not to follow after the world's advice on the afternoon talk shows or in the supermarket tabloids. The woman or man who is going to be happiest in life is the person who *delights* (that word says it all) in the law of the Lord, His Word.

For the one who delights in her Dad's Word

> shall be like a tree planted by the rivers of water, that brings forth its fruit in its season, whose leaf also shall not wither; and whatever he does shall prosper. The ungodly are not so, but are like the chaff which the wind drives away. Therefore the ungodly shall not stand in the judgment, nor sinners in the congregation of the righteous. For the LORD knows the way of the righteous, but the way of the ungodly shall perish (Psalm 1:3-6).

The second chapter of Proverbs takes this concept a little further and helps us understand how God uses His Word to guide us. Solomon writes:

> My son, if you receive my words, and treasure my commands within you, so that you incline your ear to wisdom, and apply your heart to understanding; yes, if you cry out for discernment, and lift up your voice for understanding, if you seek her as silver, and search for her as for hidden treasures, *then you will understand the fear of the LORD, and find the knowledge of God.* For the Lord gives wisdom (Proverbs 2:1-6, emphasis added).

Your Dad loves to guide you.

> For the LORD gives wisdom; from His mouth come knowledge and understanding; He stores up sound wisdom for the upright; He is a shield to those who walk uprightly; He guards the paths of justice, and preserves the way of His saints. Then you will understand righteousness and justice, equity and every good path (Proverbs 2:6-9).

51

As you take in and treasure your Dad's guidance, as you truly desire to possess it and know what's best for you, then He will give you His guidance. He'll give you exactly what you seek.

Consider Proverbs 2:10-13. What a tremendous statement is made there about the way God guides through His Word!

> When wisdom enters your heart, and knowledge is pleasant to your soul, discretion will preserve you; understanding will keep you, to deliver you from the way of evil, from the man who speaks perverse things, from those who leave the paths of uprightness to walk in the ways of darkness.

When wisdom enters your heart, when you delight in your Dad's guidance so that it truly is a pleasure to you, you begin to say to yourself, "Wait a minute! This Book isn't trying to rain on my parade. It isn't a giant 'NO' to everything I ever wanted to do. It isn't something I need to be afraid of or something designed to condemn me. Why, this Book opens up an unbelievable understanding of life and explains how I can live in such a way that I will be truly happy!"

When your Dad's guidance becomes that exciting to you, then He says, "Discretion will preserve you." Please note the word *discretion*. It's critical.

In its most basic sense, discretion means choosing to follow God's guidance. It presupposes the ability to discern the difference between God's best and anything else, and then to choose only God's best.

Adam and Eve had a choice in the garden. They

knew God's best. He told them. There was nothing fuzzy in their conversation with God, nothing left to chance. But they were unwilling to exercise discretion. Though they knew what their Dad had said, they chose to depart from His guidance. And we all have been paying for that lack of discretion ever since!

As you follow your Dad's guidance in the Word, "discretion will preserve you, and understanding will keep you, to deliver you from the way of evil from the man who speaks perverse things. . . ." All because God is guiding and directing you.

A second resource your Dad gives to guide you is His Holy Spirit. John 16:8 tells us that when the Holy Spirit comes, He will convict the world of sin, righteousness, and judgment. The thirteenth verse says He will also "guide you into all truth; for He will not speak on His own authority, but whatever He hears He will speak." "He will glorify Me," Jesus said, because "He will take of what is Mine and declare it to you."

How does the Spirit guide you? For one thing, He helps you understand when you are moving into problem areas. It's almost as if an invisible finger taps you on the shoulder and a voice says, "Are you sure that you want to do this? Are you sure you would want to have this reported in the local paper? Are you sure you would like to see this flashed on the evening news? Are you sure this is something that will make you proud and make other people respect you? Are you sure this is something that will build you up? Are you sure this is going to get you where you want to be?" In convicting God's kids of sin, the Spirit enables them to see when they are toying with disaster.

At the same time He does this, He brings an

understanding of God's best. Remember, the Spirit not only convicts the world of sin, but also of righteousness. Even as you see what is *not* good for you, He helps us to understand what *is*. Then, because He lives within you, He encourages you to go after what is best with everything you have.

A third resource God uses to guide His kids is His people. When God is your Dad, you become part of a very large family. You have lots of brothers and sisters who are on your side. You don't have to worry about sibling rivalry because God has put those brothers and sisters in your life to help guide you and assist in your growth.

Many times, those who haven't had a dad to guide them have learned to trust no one but themselves. They find it difficult to trust anybody. They are fearful that if they open themselves up to others, if they become vulnerable, they will get hurt or let down, maybe even crushed.

Is that you? Do you feel like that? If so, unless I miss my guess, you've come to find that trusting only yourself doesn't work very well. It hasn't brought you a great deal of happiness. You know quite well that the Lone Ranger is, more than anything, *alone*.

God wants you to understand that He hasn't created you to function that way. He has brought brothers and sisters into your life who can help you grow to maturity, who can help you in the process of growing up. He provides people who will weep with you when you weep and rejoice with you when you rejoice (*see* Romans 12:15). He provides people who will provoke you to love and good works (*see* Hebrews 10:24), who will hang in there and say, "Come on, we can do better than that!" He will provide people who will love you unconditionally, just as Jesus said in John 13:34: "Love one another; as I have loved you." As God has accepted you and as He has been there for you, so does He provide people to be there for you, too.

As it is presented in Ephesians 4, the major focus of the church is your health. There is nobody more important to your Dad than you are. He loves you so much that He has given you a whole flock of brothers and sisters to enable you to understand and live out His guidance.

A final resource God uses to guide you is the unique gifts and abilities He places in you. You have gifts that are special to you. Through these gifts, God not only guides you, but He builds up the rest of His family as well.

You may have a prophetic gift, for example. You seem to have a clear understanding of God's truth and an intense desire to declare it. As you do, God gives guidance not only to you but to His whole family.

Or you may have a gift of administration. You are able to discern how His people need to be organized and have the wherewithal to make it happen. This is not an effort for you, but seems to come quite naturally. Again, God guides as this gift is exercised appropriately.

Maybe you have a gift of worship. You are drawn to worship God in a deep way, and as you share that gift with others, they are enabled to go deeper in their worship as well. As you put your gift to work, God guides you and those around you.

All God's kids have been especially gifted by Him. You are no exception—nobody is more important to your Dad than you are. That is why He has made certain to present you with unique gifts. He guides you through them and builds up and encourages His family. As you begin to exercise the gifts He has placed in your life and follow the guidance He gives you, not only will you be happier and more complete, but all those brothers and sisters with whom you have been joined will be as well. God gives powerful resources to guide His kids.

Guidance For Those Who Never Had It

You may be like one of my friends whom I described earlier. You may feel as though you have been shortchanged. Because your earthly father never guided you, you have a tough time believing that your heavenly Father will be any different. When it comes to guidance, you may feel as though you've been left out completely.

Now hear this! This is truth straight from your perfect Dad. Because He loves you, He guides you. He desires to have a hand in directing every move of your life. That is why He says to you in His Word, "Trust in the LORD with all your heart, and lean not on your own understanding; in all your ways acknowledge Him, and He shall direct your paths" (Proverbs 3:5-6).

Open yourself to your Dad's guidance. See for yourself the incredible foundation that His guidance provides for you. Let it set the pace for the way in which you relate to others, especially as you are called to guide them. Regardless of what may be missing in your past, let His truth be the foundation for a new present and future. Never lose sight of this fact:

Because your Dad loves you, He guides you!

CHAPTER FOUR

My Dad Corrects Me

At the heart of growing up is something that makes most of us uncomfortable. It was especially uncomfortable when connected to an infamous phrase: "Just wait until your father gets home!" What is it?

Correction.

Somehow, at certain times, the thought that our dad was about to walk through the door didn't lighten our days or fill us with exquisite joy. For some of us, even today the thought of correction strikes terror in our hearts. We cringe just to think of it.

I almost used the term *discipline* for this chapter, but that word has such negative connotations for many people that they can only see it as harmful. *Correction*, on the other hand, suggests a positive thrust. Everybody needs correction.

But whether we need it or not, many of us recoil from this part of the growth process. Consider, for instance, those who have been physically brutalized in the name of correction.

Correction Gone Haywire

Recently a two-year-old Oregon girl was killed by her father. Trying to discipline her one day, he kicked her so hard in the stomach that he ruptured her intestine. Peritonitis set in, and though the family lived only one minute away from an emergency medical clinic, he didn't get around to taking her in until her little body had turned completely purple some twenty-two hours later. By the time they got her to the hospital, it was too late. There was nothing that could be done. She died.

An autopsy found that this little girl's ribs had been broken on three separate occasions in the month prior to her death. Her dad evidently felt the best way to administer discipline was by hitting and kicking and any other form of physical abuse he could think of. He was tried for his daughter's death and found guilty. I guess it wasn't that hard to determine that a thirty-seven-year-old man just might have the upper hand on a twenty-three-month-old toddler.

I don't know about you, but whenever I see a story like that about to hit the TV screen I switch the channel. I can't handle that stuff. When I read about it in the newspaper and I realize where the article is headed, I quit reading and move to the sports page. Indeed, you may be feeling that way by reading this!

I had a similar response when I was preparing

material for this book. Hundreds of people graciously responded to a questionnaire I put together that asked about their relationship with their dads. Many of those relationships were horrid. From time to time I couldn't help but yell out, "No, you can't do that!" But, of course, they could do that and they did do that, and there was nothing I could do about it.

It's easy to assume that brutality only happens to strangers in distant places. But that assumption would be frightfully wrong. Discipline degenerates into brutality every day in places you'd hardly expect. People you sit next to every Sunday in church are scarred by it; so are friends and acquaintances. It's all too likely that people you're very close to simply have never told you some of the things that devastated their growing-up years.

Tammy grew up with a dad whose form of discipline was to beat her unmercifully. No matter what the infraction, he beat her. Normally he whipped her with a leather strap or with an actual whip. Whatever she did—whether she was home five minutes late from school or didn't have dinner started by whatever timetable he had in mind at the moment—he would take out his instrument of torture and beat her until his arm got tired.

He didn't restrict his beatings to her. He inflicted this punishment on every member of the family. As a consequence, every single kid left home just as soon as they were old enough. Tammy's time came when she was sixteen. That's when her dad beat her so viciously that she was unable to walk for two days. When she had recovered enough to rise from her bed, she said to her mother, "That's it. I'm out of here. As soon as I can move my legs decently, I'm gone." The very next day when her dad was at work, she and her mother packed up and left, never to return again.

Sharon's story is not much different. Her stepdad entered her life when she was six. She was spared the beatings at that tender age, but only because her mother bore the full brunt of his anger.

That all changed when Sharon's mom died. At nine years of age, Sharon moved into the role of mom for her brother (eight years old) and for her two half-sisters (two years of age and eight months). Recalling those nightmarish years, Sharon wrote this: "I also inherited the role of being beaten and sexually abused. My dad threatened me with death if I told. Not until I was sixteen did I get brave enough to call the authorities. He spent time in prison. He confessed. The restraints that he used for the beatings were all the evidence the authorities needed."

Think about that—shackled and beaten by her own stepdad. Words can't express the horror. But just in case anybody's thinking that this is something that dads do only to little girls, let me tell you about Bob.

Bob had what today would be considered a learning disability. School was difficult for him. No matter the subject, it just didn't sink in. It's not that he didn't want to learn, he simply could not process the information. The mere mention of an upcoming test would send tremors down his spine.

Even as a little tyke, Bob brought home report cards filled with failure. All F's. And Bob knew the drill that was coming next.

First, his dad would beat him with an electric fry pan cord, just thin enough to cut through the skin. When that was finished, Bob's room was stripped of everything extraneous (basically everything except the bed) and Bob was placed on a stool in the middle of the room, handed an armload of school books, and forced to sit there for six weeks, non-stop, day and night. Somehow he was supposed to become what he wasn't and transform himself into a world-class scholar.

If that didn't work (and of course it never did), his dad had other methods. Sometimes he would throw Bob into a bathtub filled with scalding water. At other times he would get so mad he'd beat Bob with his fists—pommel him in the face just to vent his frustration and get out his anger.

The Positive Side of Correction

With a backdrop like that—which, by the way, is not nearly as unusual as you might think—is it any wonder that some people can't help but see red flags when anybody mentions the word *correction?* And yet the truth is, apart from correction, none of us will ever become what we were meant to be. We simply cannot become mature or complete or whole without correction.

Why not? Because none of us is born perfect. Whether we're talking about ethics or behavioral skills or styles, none of us is born having it all together. The only way we can get it together is through correction by someone who loves us enough to shape us and mold us in a loving and wise way. Even precious metals become purified only as they are refined through fire. The same is true with people, only their "fire" takes the shape of correction.

But I know what some of you are thinking: *Is it possible to have discipline or correction that builds up rather than beats up?*

61

Yes, it is—if the one administering it is a perfect Dad.

As practiced by the God of all creation, your perfect Dad, correction can actually be a beautiful thing. I didn't say pleasant! I said beautiful. As the child of a perfect Dad, you are corrected in such a way that you are built up and shaped and helped to become everything you were meant to be. Unlike many earthly dads, your perfect Dad always and without exception has your best interests at heart. Thus, while His correction isn't exactly fun, it always enables you to grow into the mature man or woman you really want to be.

What Is God's Correction Like?

What does God's correction look like? What does it feel like? How is it expressed and how does it demonstrate real love? The twelfth chapter of Hebrews gives a terrifically helpful description of it. Of course, no one section of Scripture can provide a definitive explanation either of God's correction or how God's people ought to respond to it. But this passage really does give us some basic handles to understand how our Dad corrects us and how He would have us learn from it.

Here's the passage:

And you have forgotten the exhortation which speaks to you as to sons: "My son, do not despise the chastening [or correction] of the LORD, nor be discouraged when you are rebuked by Him; for whom the LORD loves, He [corrects], and scourges [or spanks] every son whom He receives."

If you endure [correction], God deals with

you as with sons; for what son is there whom a father does not [correct]? But if you are without [correction], of which all have become partakers, then you are illegitimate and not sons.

Furthermore, we have had human fathers who corrected us, and we paid them respect. Shall we not much more readily be in subjection to the Father of spirits and live? For they indeed for a few days [corrected] us as seemed best to them, but He for our profit, that we may be partakers of His holiness.

Now no [correction] seems to be joyful for the present, but grievous; nevertheless, afterward it yields the peaceable fruit of righteousness to those who have been trained [or corrected] by it (Hebrews 12:5-11).

This passage teaches us several things about God's correction. First, because God is a Dad who loves his children, He corrects them.

For Whom the Lord Loves . . .

Let me make this more personal. When God is your Dad, He loves you. Because He loves you, He corrects you. Don't fly by verse 6. It sets the pace for everything: "For whom the LORD loves, He [corrects] and [spanks] every son whom He receives." (That bit about "spanks" is my own translation. I think it better captures the thought for modern ears. You get that for free.)

Please note the order here: For whom the Lord loves, He corrects. That order is exceedingly important. It's the foundation for everything else. A number of modern translations invert the order and read something like, "The Lord disciplines those whom He loves." That's unfortunate. The author of this statement put it in a particular order for a reason, and the original text has "love" first.

Love always precedes everything else. It precedes discipline. It precedes correction. If you were brutalized by harsh discipline, it's because love did not precede it. Whenever correction is expressed outside the context of love, it's outside the will of the Lord. It is not God's style to correct apart from love. Whom the Lord loves, He corrects.

The Bible insists that proper correction demonstrates love. It doesn't somehow destroy it. But if that's true, you may be wondering: *then what is proper correction?* I maintain that proper correction occurs when someone does something *to* you because they want to do something *for* you.

They don't do something to you just because they are angry. They don't do something to you just because they are frustrated. They don't do something to you just to get your attention. They do something to you because they want to build you up.

A parent should never correct without a clear sense of how the correction enables her child to become more mature, more complete, more whole. And, of course, she never corrects except when her child is missing the mark, getting off the track of maturity, wandering from becoming what God most desires. Correction is to enable that child to get back on track, to get a little further down the road where God wants him to be.

Whenever parents stop doing something *to* a child because they desire to do something *for* that child, they step across the line from correction to abuse. And God stands immovably against that turn of events.

The Flip Side of Training

Correction is simply the other side of training. The word translated in Hebrews 12 as *correction* is translated in 90 percent of its other New Testament appearances as "training" or "instructing" or "guiding." Correction is simply the flip side of training. Correction is another way in which we are trained or instructed or guided. Correction based on anger is completely out of God's will. Such correction cannot fulfill the purpose for which it was intended.

God nails that down clearly in the Word. Ephesians 6:4 reads, "And you, fathers, do not provoke your children to wrath, but bring them up in the training [or correction] and admonition of the Lord."

Don't provoke your children to wrath. Just because you're hacked off, don't do things which embitter them. Acting out of wrath negates the expression of God's life and God's love. He wants to see people built up in His life and in His love. That's why He says to do only those things that will enable little ones to be brought up in the life of the Lord.

A corollary text is found in Colossians 3:21. "Fathers," it says, "do not provoke [or embitter] your children, lest they become discouraged." Don't vent your anger on your kids. Always correct with a view toward shaping, directing, and guiding them in the things of the Lord. If you don't, you can expect to cause horrible problems later on. Provoking your kids is not an expression of God's love or God's life and it is clearly not an option.

When God does something *to* His people it is always because He desires to do something *for* His people. Therefore, He is never going to do something *to* you unless he wants to do something *for* you to facilitate your growth.

Permissive Means Illegitimate

Back to Hebrews. In the seventh and eighth verses of chapter 12, notice how God's correction demonstrates His love. "What son is there whom a father does not [correct]?" the writer asks. Then he adds, "if you are without [correction], of which all have become partakers, then you are illegitimate." Illegitimate means you aren't truly a son. So if there is no correction, that means there is no relationship. If there is no correction, there's no concern.

This text speaks directly to the problem of parents who become too permissive. They often become so because of their own upbringing. Maybe they were beaten or regularly made to feel like dirt. For a variety of reasons they have such an aversion to discipline that they don't correct their children.

But do you see what that does? Instead of helping their children to become mature, they help them to become monsters. They are monsters to themselves and monsters to everyone around them. It simply is not helpful to them or to society to refrain from guiding and shaping children by proper correction.

As stated earlier, correction presupposes that someone has moved a bit off the track. It's the parent's job to help them get back on track. And helping to define the track and get back on is what correction is all about.

Because your Dad loves you, He corrects you. That's the underlying principle. He wants to help you become everything you were designed to be. He will never, ever exert discipline capriciously just because He's ticked off at you. He will always do it to make you stronger, to make you better, to give you a life that is richer and fuller. Because your Dad loves you, He corrects you.

God's Methods of Correction

Your Dad corrects you in several identifiable ways, ways that parallel His methods of guidance. That's no accident—God's involvement with you is not arbitrary or haphazard. He coordinates His efforts on your behalf to make your life full and rich and whole. Your perfect Dad orchestrates all the events of your life in order to help you become more like His Son.

What are the ways in which He corrects you? He corrects you through His Word. He corrects you through His Spirit. He corrects you through His people and He corrects you through circumstances. Let's take a look at each one of those.

First, He corrects you through His Word. Second Timothy 3:16-17 says, "All Scripture is given by inspiration of God, and is profitable for doctrine, for reproof, for correction, for instruction in righteousness, that the man of God may be complete, thoroughly equipped for every good work."

God's Word is God's Word. It's God breathed. This is not just another book. This is not just an interesting theory. This is reality. And one of the major functions of God's Word is correction and instruction in righteousness. What does that accomplish? "That the man of God may be complete, thoroughly equipped for every good work."

Many times in my own life the Word has helped

me to come face-to-face with attitudes or actions that did not honor God or help me. I had to do some radical surgery to change those things. How did I do it? Through God's Word.

Early in my ministry a church member pointed out to me some things about my style that didn't exactly line up with the character of Christ. He was certain that God wanted me to work on them.

Outwardly, I received his comments graciously. Inwardly, I was seething. *Just who in the world does this idiot think HE is, anyway?* I thought. *Why, his marriage is a mess. He's struggling with booze. One of his kids has gone over the edge. So what makes him think he has a right to correct me? If he were a different person, maybe his comments would be worth listening to!* So I dismissed what he had to say.

The next day as I turned to my daily devotions, his words came back like a flood. At that point in my reading I was in Numbers 22, the story of Balaam. Remember Balaam, the man who was so caught up in his own agenda that he couldn't hear God? Finally, in order to get his attention, the Lord spoke to him through a donkey!

It's my guess that the donkey didn't smell so hot. His morals may have been questionable. He wasn't listed on anybody's "Who's Who" list. Yet God, in His infinite wisdom, spoke to Balaam through the donkey.

As I read that story, it was as if God jabbed me in the ribs with His elbow and said, "Get it?" I did.

God does use His Word to help us see how we are missing out on His best. He corrects by means of His Word.

Second, He corrects by means of His Spirit. John 16:8 reminds us that one function of the Holy Spirit is to convict us of sin. How does He do that? Among other things, by pricking our consciences so that we'll know the difference between right and wrong and recognize when we're moving into situations far from God's best for us. The Holy Spirit works within, through that inner voice, to let us know where we are headed.

When He does so, we have a decision to make. Are we going to override what the Spirit is saying and go ahead and do what we want to do anyway? Will we choose to sing, "I Did It My Way"? Or are we going to listen to that still, small voice and steer our ship back into safe harbors?

One evening a pastor friend of mine was leading a Bible study of single adults. Just as he began his lesson, one of the regulars in the group arrived late and quickly took a seat. At that very moment, as my friend eyed the new arrival, he felt impressed by God's Spirit that this young man had just been involved in sexual immorality.

As you might well imagine, my friend was blown away. What in the world was he supposed to do with this information? What if he were wrong? What if his thoughts were more a function of hot salsa than Holy Spirit?

After the meeting concluded and folks were enjoying refreshments, at an opportune time my friend got alone with this young man. As gently as he could, he brought up the subject. "You know, Tim," he began, "I had a most unusual experience during the study tonight. Just as you walked into the room, I thought that the Holy Spirit told me that you were struggling with sexual immorality. Is there any truth to that?"

You could have knocked the poor guy over with a feather. Hardly had the words left my friend's lips than this fellow broke down crying. As they moved outside for a more private setting, he confessed some deep difficulties he'd been having with sexual immorality, the last episode of which had occurred that very afternoon.

Through it all, God was able to do some major rescuing, cleansing, purifying, restoring, and building. Thank God that He corrects by means of His Spirit! If He didn't, just think how devastating the consequences could be!

Third, the Lord corrects us by means of His people. Hebrews 10:24-25 says, "Let us consider one another in order to stir up [or provoke] love and good works, not forsaking the assembling of ourselves together, as is the manner of some, but exhorting one another, and so much the more as you see the Day approaching."

I couldn't begin to tell you how many times I have talked with people who have said, "Oh, I'm a Christian, but I don't go to church. I'm really not into that church stuff—organized religion and that sort of thing. I think as long as I have a relationship with God and as long as I believe in Jesus, that's quite sufficient."

It's certainly quite interesting, but it's also quite wrong. God insists that He intends to correct us by means of His people. It is only as we are in relationship with people over time that we can be held accountable for the direction of our lives. People who know us know the direction we are headed as well as the direction we ought to be headed. As they love us and act in accordance with God's Word—as they speak the truth in love—they put their arms around us and bring us back to where God wants us to be. That is one of the most basic reasons for the church. That is why God believes it is so important that we continue in fellowship. In church.

Time and again I have seen people whose lives, spiritually and in all other ways, have disintegrated. They have removed themselves from fellowship with God's people and so were not able to be corrected or admonished. Sometimes they leave the church just when they need it most. Someone confronts them on an issue and they respond, "Hey, I don't need to listen to this. And I don't need to listen to you. I'm not receiving any of this. I'm out of here." I've seen a lot of human wreckage just because people took exactly this attitude.

God corrects by means of His people.

Last, God corrects by means of circumstance. That's one of the hardest things for us to handle, yet it's one of the most typical ways in which He corrects. A good place to see how this works is found in the fifth chapter of Isaiah. The whole chapter is a warning to ancient Israel that unless they turn from their wickedness, God would discipline the nation. He uses the picture of a vineyard to represent the nation. In the fifth verse, the Lord says, "And now, please let Me tell you what I will do to My vineyard: I will take away its hedge, and it shall be burned; and break down its wall, and it shall be trampled down."

The Lord owns everything that exists. He created it. He put it together. And He can jolly well do with it whatever He desires. Many times we operate without the knowledge that we are continually protected by the Lord from all kinds of things. He puts a hedge of protection around us and deflects all kinds of struggles and difficulties and problems that we would otherwise experience. We may be oblivious to it, but He does it nonetheless.

The problem arises when we continue to make decisions to move apart from Him. He will work to get our attention. He will work through His Word, He will work through His Spirit, and He will work through His people. He only resorts to severe correction as a last option. That's what Jeremiah meant when he wrote:

> For the Lord will not cast off forever. Though He causes grief, yet He will show compassion according to the multitude of His mercies. *For He does not afflict willingly, nor grieve the children of men* (Lamentations 3:31-33, emphasis added).

But finally, if we reject all of His lighter means, we give Him no other option. He removes the protective hedge from our lives and we are exposed to the natural consequences of our bad decisions. If you don't think He does this, I suggest you read your Bible again.

One of the best examples of this is Israel. Why were His people taken captive by Babylon? For centuries God sent to them prophets saying, "Don't do this. Don't do this. Here's My life. Walk with Me. Come with Me. This is how it's meant to be lived." But His people said, "We're not having any of it." Finally He lifted His hedge of protection and His people were taken into captivity.

Why did He allow that to happen? Because He

loved them. He never forsook them. He never wrote them off or walked away from them. He loved them through the whole process in order to bring them back to Himself.

The same thing is true with Jerusalem. Time and again God spoke to its people and repeatedly they refused to listen. Jesus wept over the city: "Jerusalem, Jerusalem, the one who kills the prophets and stones those who are sent to her! How often I wanted to gather your children together, as a hen gathers her chicks under her wings, but you were not willing! See! Your house is left to you desolate" (Matthew 23:37-38).

In A.D. 70 the Romans burned the city to the ground, exactly as Jesus had predicted.

There are times when God removes the protective barrier around His children and allows them to experience the consequences of their decisions. But even then, it is because He loves them and desires wholeheartedly to bring them back to Himself. He wants to grow them up in His life, to prompt them to look to Him, to trust Him, to walk with Him. Circumstances can be a hard lesson, but they are one form of God's correction.

Don't Despise God's Correction

It's easy to despise correction or be discouraged by it—especially if you were once disciplined in a brutal or hurtful fashion. If the correction you've received has been harmful and nothing else, you might find yourself reacting to God's correction in exactly the two ways that Hebrews 12:5 warns us against: "My son, do not despise the [correction] of the LORD, nor be discouraged when you are rebuked by Him."

Some folks despise correction. When it comes, they stiffen their necks and say, "You just try and see if you can break me down. You just try and see if you can correct me. You just try your best—it's not going to happen." They're like Pharaoh: "Okay, hit me with another plague and we'll just see what's going to happen." Some people despise any kind of correction and do anything they can to get away from it.

Others react much differently. They become totally discouraged by it: "Oh man, I can't do anything right." They withdraw and become fearful of people, of God, of God's people, of His Word, fearful of everything.

That is why it is so important to get back to where we began. God's love precedes everything. Don't despise correction nor be discouraged, because whom the Lord loves, He corrects. What son or daughter is there whom a father does not correct? In fact, if you are without correction, then you are illegitimate. You are not His children at all.

It truly can be said of God that His correction hurts Him much more than it hurts us. He loves us so much that He wishes it didn't have to get to that. Remember Lamentations 3:33? God will never do something *to* you unless He deeply desires to do something *for* you.

Wrap your minds around this! *Because your Dad loves you, He corrects you.* He loves you so much, He neither wants to see you destroyed nor does He want to see you self-destruct.

Don't despise His correction or be discouraged by it. Rather, rejoice in it, because through it He is helping you to become everything you were designed to be.

Because your Dad loves you, He corrects you.

CHAPTER FIVE

My Dad Provides for Me

One of the greatest things my own dad ever gave me was a base of stability and security. It was such a given that I never thought to call it into question. I never was anxious about what the next day would bring. Of course, I had the usual kinds of kid concerns—will I be able to survive high school? Get into the college I want? Find the right job? But I never once worried about the basics: food, shelter, clothing, my folks' relationship as husband and wife. Those were certainties for me and they created a base on which to build my life.

It never occurred to me that something might happen that could terminate this operation. All I knew was that I enjoyed a phenomenal base of security and stability.

Now that doesn't mean I had everything that I ever wanted. Far from it. My dad was never in a position to give that to me. But when it came to the things I truly required, I never had a need that Dad was either unable or unwilling to meet.

He reaffirmed this stability and security through the consistency of his life. He was absolutely and totally predictable. If my dad were alive today and I were to see him, I know exactly what he'd say to me: "Hi, Willie." If I were to walk into my dad's shop, I could tell you exactly what song he would be singing and probably which part of the song he would be on. If I hadn't seen my dad for a year or two years or five years, I could tell you exactly what his shoes would look like. I could tell you what time he got up in the morning. I could almost tell you what he did every hour of the day. And I'll bet that within five minutes I could tell you what time he went to bed that night.

Everything in his life was so rock solid, so consistent, so predictable, that it formed a tremendous base for life. I knew that he wouldn't love me today and stop loving me tomorrow. I knew that he wouldn't care for my needs today and then withhold that same care tomorrow. I knew there were certainties in life that were a function of being a part of his family.

Counting on Stability

It is a wonderful thing to have a life built on that kind of stability. I was telling somebody not long ago that I'd have to make instability a project if it were ever to become a part of my life. It's fabulous to have that kind of foundation for life.

A whole lot of people share such a terrific heritage. Nancy wrote to tell me about her adopted dad:

"Dad needn't be your biological father. I've never met my biological father. My dad married my mom nearly thirty-three years ago when I was an infant. She was single with six small children. And they are still married. My dad is a very giving man. He provided all of our needs and allowed my mom to stay home. He was a hard-working carpenter. We weren't rich, but we thought we were. He never made us feel that we weren't really his kids. As a matter of fact, I didn't even know until I was older. He was the type who would bring home a candy bar for us in his lunch pail on Fridays. He allowed me to buy a horse with my berry-picking money and taught me how to work."

Judy's letter went on for pages and pages and warmed my soul. I know it will yours as well. Let me lift out one vignette about her childhood that gives you an indication of the love in which she felt enveloped:

My childhood was fantastic, heaping with love and attention. My dad and I did lots of fun things together. He allowed me to be a child, never expecting more than I was capable of. He truly understood how kids think and what kids really want to do to have fun. And he had as much fun, if not more, as we did! He knew how to play.

My dad made the biggest and best kites in the whole world. Every size and lots of shapes, including box kites. The tails went on forever. The string was endless—not just a ball, but wrapped around a piece of board or stick of some sort so you could hang on and still release more string. I can remember my dad and I and the beautiful green fields scattered with splashes of orange poppies. He'd get the kite flying and then he'd say, "Okay, now it's all up to you. Are you ready?" And then he'd secure my hands on the stick and he'd let out more and more string. Our kites flew so high they looked like little specks in the sky. And then, when they'd be up so far, he would tell me that if he didn't hang onto me, I'd be flying, too. So he'd sit down behind me and hang onto my legs. Maybe he exaggerated just a little, but I believed him.

And then there was my scooter. Oh boy! Mine was so classy. My dad made it from an all-wood box. Made the front of it with the hollow side facing me and then wooden handlebars angled out and the box was secured onto a board just long enough for your knees or your foot. It rolled on metal skate wheels. My dad really spruced mine up. I had extra wheels! And all over the front of the box he decorated it with what seemed like hundreds of bottle caps. I loved it!

Growing up in an environment like that, you couldn't help but feel a sense of stability, of security. No matter what was going on in the world, even though it might be falling apart, you were safe because your dad was there. Probably tomorrow he'd take you out to fly that kite again. Or maybe he'd make a scooter or something else that would make next week even more fun than the last.

It is a wonderful thing to have a dad who provides you with a base of security and stability. It allows you to grow up without taking on all the concerns that will be yours soon enough. It gives you a clear example to follow. More than that, it gives you a foundation of security on which to build a life of real strength.

Unfortunately, not everyone has such a foundation. Don certainly didn't. Speaking about his dad, he said, "When he would come home from the bars he would beat up my mom all night and wreck the house."

In other cases, if folks once had a secure foundation, they feel as if it slipped away from them. Some people's sense of security passed away with their dads. Others who never had a resident dad often have little concept of what a life of security or stability would look like. Still others suffered through home lives that were so unbelievably fouled up that they can't imagine how to establish for themselves a life of security. They think it's too late. When it should have been there for them, it wasn't, and they've spent their whole lives trying to put it together. Frankly, it hasn't worked well.

Your Unshakable Base of Security

How comforting it is to realize that your perfect Dad will provide rock-solid security and stability! It doesn't make any difference whether you've had it and lost it or whether you never had it in the first place. God is committed to building for all of His kids a base of stability and security on which to build their lives.

That doesn't mean your life will be easy or that you will have everything you want. But it does mean that despite your struggles, you will have a deep, inner sense of security and stability. You'll know that your Dad has everything in control. He has promised to exert all His power on your behalf, and He always keeps His promises. Even though you go through tough and trying times, you're going to win this battle!

79

You've got a Dad who will make certain of that.

Paul had a great deal to say about this in the fourth chapter of Philippians. He develops it beautifully. Here's the passage:

> Be anxious for nothing, but in everything by prayer and supplication, with thanksgiving, let your requests be made known to God; and the peace of God, which surpasses all under-standing, will guard your hearts and minds through Christ Jesus (Philippians 4:6-7).

Because your Dad loves you, He provides a stable base for you so that you need not be anxious about anything. It's stated here as a command: "Be anxious for nothing."

By definition, anxiety is not a good thing. It means to be unduly concerned about something, to be worried and fretful. We all know that concern, in and of itself, is not bad. But when concern gets out of control, when it mutates into anxiety and you worry about situations over which you have no control, it can be deadly.

The word translated "anxious" comes from a root which means "to divide" or "to separate." An anxious person is a double-minded person. He becomes so preoccupied with worrisome possibilities that he can't cope with reality. He is so consumed by what isn't that he can't handle what is.

The first church I pastored had a congregation of about twenty-four adults. Every Sunday morning at eleven o'clock I'd be standing at the front door, strain-ing and looking for who *wasn't* there. Meanwhile, the faithful twenty-four busied themselves in the back-ground. Instead of spending my time with who *was* there and cultivating those relationships, I was fretting and stewing over people who didn't even exist.

That is exactly what Paul is warning us about. He doesn't want us to be distracted like that. He doesn't want us to be unduly concerned about things over which we have no control. That's why the apostle can say so confidently, "Be anxious for nothing." God wants to give us a base of stability that frees us from useless worry.

Ah! But that prompts the question, "Yes, but how can you live like that, practically speaking?" Paul tells us how. He says that God provides us this base of security *as we give our worries to Him.* "Be anxious for nothing, but in everything by prayer and supplication, with thanksgiving, let your requests be made known to God."

God provides the security you need as you give your worries to Him. But you have to give Him those worries. Otherwise, they're still yours.

Think about what Jesus said in Matthew 11:28: "Come to Me, all you who labor and are heavy laden, and I will give you rest." Or what Peter said in 1 Peter 5:7: "Casting all your care upon Him, for He cares for you." God wants His kids to give to Him their struggles. God wants His sons and His daughters to give to Him whatever binds them up, the obstacles that stand in their way. And He wants to replace them with the enjoyment of simple peace in everyday living.

Saying Goodbye to Anxiety

Such peace isn't handed out once-and-for-all, however. God gives us an ongoing means to obtain it. Paul says that if we want to give God our struggles, we do it first of all through prayer.

Prayer is the simple act of communicating with God, both talking and listening. Sometimes we see prayer as a one-way street. We think it means telling God about things that are happening to us. But real prayer involves both give and take. It means not only talking to Him, but also listening to Him.

This is not necessarily an intense thing—heads bowed and eyes closed, breathing reduced to near-coma. It simply means sharing with God the give-and-take of your life. It has to happen regularly, continuously.

Look at it like this. If you're going to give Him your cares, you must have a viable relationship with Him. And you cannot have a viable relationship with God (or anyone else) apart from ongoing, honest communication.

Did you ever have a really close friend who moved away? You spent all kinds of time with this friend. You talked about everything. You had overnights together. You were inseparable. But then that friend moved and somehow, over time, your beautiful relationship deteriorated. It didn't deteriorate because you ceased liking that friend or because you didn't care anymore. It deteriorated because you didn't have the opportunity to communicate. As you both grew and changed and matured, you grew apart. Why? You never had the chance to talk about all the things that were changing in your separate worlds.

Lack of communication is the number one reason for marriages breaking down. Each spouse may be talking, but neither is listening. Without ongoing communication, no relationship is viable, let alone strong.

So it is with God. If ever you are to give Him

your cares and worries and anxieties, you must have a viable relationship with Him. And that relationship begins with prayer.

The second means of giving our anxieties to God is supplication. Supplication is a much more intense expression of prayer. It gets right down to the nitty gritty of your life. In supplication you share with God the deepest needs of your heart, the worst nightmares you've ever had, and the greatest hopes you nourish. It means baring your heart to God. You willingly lift to God your burdens and expect Him to take them away. That may include the baggage from your past. It may mean the struggles you face in the present. It may mean obstacles looming in the future.

The Problem with Living Sacrifices

It is exactly at this point where the process breaks down for most people. Either they feel God doesn't really care, or they simply won't give up their burdens. It's something like a friend of mine used to say: "It's difficult to be a living sacrifice for the Lord when I keep hopping off the altar."

It's difficult to give my concerns to God if I keep taking them back. How can I lay my burdens at His feet if I tie them to my ankles so they drag along behind me as I walk away from Him?

My observations confirm that many people don't want to give their burdens to God at all. They like to muck about in their past. They enjoy stewing on the same issues over and over, month after month, year after year. The problem is that the longer you stew in your own juices, the tougher you get—and the worse you smell.

God doesn't want that to happen. He wants His

kids to lift to Him the deepest and heaviest burdens they carry. That's what supplication is all about. Once you begin communicating with God through prayer, you move to supplication where you give these things to the Lord.

One last comment. Unless there is something hidden in the original Greek of Matthew 11:28, Jesus seems to mean exactly what He says: "Come to Me, all you who labor and are heavy laden. . . ." I don't think He was kidding. I think He meant exactly what He said. I also think Peter was inspired by the Holy Spirit to write, ". . . casting *all* your care upon Him, for He cares for you." I can see no reason to believe that He meant anything other than what He said. Can you?

The Pilgrims Had It Right

The third means to ridding yourself of anxiety is thanksgiving. Once you have given your concerns to the Lord, you need to thank Him that He has taken them from you.

The most natural response you can make for His tender care is to say, "Thank You." "Thank You so much! These were so heavy, I couldn't carry them. A horribly heavy burden has been lifted from my chest. Oh, thank You!"

When I first became a Christian, I was overwhelmed that not only did God love me and accept me, but He also took the junk out of my life as soon as I gave it to Him. I was so overwhelmed that I couldn't do anything but say "thank you" in every way I knew how. To this day I consider it a genuine privilege to be able to serve the Lord. It's just one more way of saying *thank you*.

It feels so good to know that you can give away

84

the very burdens that otherwise would crush you. Your perfect Dad will take them from you and carry them for you. You don't have to labor under their weight anymore!

You begin to give away your anxieties through communication in prayer. You deepen it through supplication, by giving God your heart's cry. You then expand it through the process of thanksgiving. Finally, Paul says, you wrap it all up by developing the relationship to such a degree that you give Him all your requests. That's the fourth thing stated in Philippians 4.

No Request Is Too Small

Eventually, you come to the point where you feel free to communicate even the little things, the seemingly meaningless aspects of your life. I've talked to scores of people who have told me, "Well, I don't think God would be very interested in my needs. I think He's pretty busy with world hunger and disease and the horrible problems of the developing nations. He's booked with the big questions of war and peace and all of those issues. I don't think He has time to be concerned about issues of mine. They aren't that big of a deal in the grand sweep of things."

Let me tell you something. If Matthew 10:30 is true when it says, "The very hairs of your head are all numbered"—and speaking from great personal experience, I know you may lose most of those—then God must care about whatever concerns you. However big, however little. He asks you to bring those requests to Him that He might respond accordingly.

The net result of giving your concerns to your perfect Dad is that you will enjoy His peace. "The peace of God, which surpasses all understanding, will

guard your hearts and minds through Christ Jesus"
(Philippians 4:7, emphasis added).

From God's perspective this isn't a guess, it's a given. The language is clear. His peace will be yours. You will have a sense of stability and security no matter what in the world is going on. No matter what you may have been through or what you are facing today, you will have His peace and the utter certainty that your Dad is actively involved in your life.

Say "Abbbbbb"

I love the statement God makes in Psalm 81. In the tenth verse, He says, "Open your mouth wide, and I will fill it."

Open your life wide to your perfect Dad and He will enfold you in His arms and establish you in the fullness of His peace. His peace will exceed anything you can imagine. It will be better than the security and stability provided by the greatest dad in human history. It will be bigger than anything you can conjure up. It will be so great you won't be able to comprehend it.

You won't need to sweat the small things anymore. Why not? Because your Dad has everything in control. His peace will be actively guarded by no less than Jesus Christ Himself. That's exactly what the text says. "And the peace of God, which surpasses all understanding, will guard your hearts and minds through Christ Jesus." Christ Jesus will stand as guard, as watchman, as sentinel upon your heart.

As you struggle with feelings of bitterness or depression or whatever, He will replace them with peace. He will stand as a guard on your heart and your mind. As your thoughts turn negative or unwholesome or compulsive, He will replace them with God's peace. Through Jesus, your Dad will establish His peace in your life in every way possible.

It's Your Turn Now

Now comes the hard part. What are you going to do about it? The question is not whether you have a Dad who wants to give you stability and security. The question is, are you going to allow Him to?

God doesn't want merely to be your Dad. He wants to be actively involved in every area of your life. He especially wants to be involved in giving you this base of security and peace. He wants you to move confidently into every arena of your life, assured that He will do a new work in you. He wants you to be able to go through every kind of situation, even difficult ones, knowing that He is right there with you and that He will bring you through and strengthen you in the process. He wants you to live each day knowing that because He is your Dad, He provides you with stability and security.

But for this to happen with you, you must do something about it. The ball is in your court. It's up to you.

What's next in your life? What will it be for you? A life filled with worry, stress, anxiety, and concern over things which you have no control? Or a life that rests firmly on the peace of God?

It really shouldn't be that hard of a question. For the truth is this:

Because your Dad loves you, He provides for you.

CHAPTER SIX

My Dad Protects Me

Everybody likes to feel safe. That's why, when you come home late at night, you turn on the lights. You're not worrying about tripping over the dog. You do it because you want to make sure that everything inside is safe.

That's also why little kids hang onto their mom's leg. Or why they snuggle under their daddy's arm—they want to feel secure and protected and know that somebody is running interference for them.

People alarm their houses for the same reason. It's why they lock their doors when they leave home or keep their keys in safe places. They want to know that everything is secure, that they are protected.

Most people feel the safest and most protected at

home. Though the storms may rage outside, inside they feel safe. Whether it's raining or snowing or crashing thunder and flashing lightening, within their castle they feel secure.

We who live in the Pacific Northwest know what it's like to be inside in the midst of a torrential downpour. As the rain sheets off your roof and over your gutters—which, unfortunately, are filled with debris since you haven't cleaned them out yet—you know what it's like to sit in your most comfortable chair and sense that everything's going to be okay. You're not getting wet because you're inside and you're safe. You put a fire in your fireplace or wood stove and feel totally secure, totally set. It's wonderful!

Though you might be heckled at school, though you may be hassled at work, as soon as you come through the doors of your house, you feel safe. You're secure and you're okay.

That's why people feel so violated when someone breaks into their home. Their sanctuary has been despoiled. The place that's supposed to make them feel safe and secure is no longer safe and secure. Panic and fear arise in their throats as they frantically wonder where they can go to find safety.

Vanishing Security

It seems to me that society is getting less and less secure. I have seen radical deterioration in this arena in just the past few years. I can't imagine how someone must feel who is twenty or thirty or forty years older than I am. When I was nine or ten, I could get on my bicycle, ride downtown, leave my bike outside the store with the kickstand down, never use a lock, and walk into the store or walk around town and not worry about someone stealing my wheels. I would come back one, two, or even five hours later and my bicycle would still be in the same place. The only thing my folks had to worry about was that I watched out for cars. If my folks weren't home when I returned, it was no big deal. The door wasn't locked, anyway. There was no reason to lock the doors. Nobody was going to come into our house unless they were invited.

How things have changed! Now we have no choice about locking the doors to our house or buying a lock for our bicycles. We just can't trust any longer that we're going to be safe and secure.

In fact, it would be wonderful if all we had to worry about was locking our doors and buying locks for our bicycles. Today we must deal with drive-by shootings, drug dealers who commandeer parks and carry on their business deals in school yards, children being abducted on their way to class, and women buying and getting permits for hand guns because they are scared to death about muggers and rapists. Each day, it seems, things are getting more unstable. The police don't even have time to deal with little things like stolen cars because there are so many bigger and more heinous crimes going on. It's hard to feel safe anymore. Even from personal threats.

Several years ago a highly unstable individual began to float in and out of our church. He believed he was destined to take over. But more than that, he was convinced I had information about a woman he was supposed to marry. Allegedly I knew not only who she was, but where she lived and worked and shopped. But, he claimed, I refused to tell him who this person was. In fact, I was teasing him. I was only giving him little hints about the identity of this woman over our radio program. Never mind that the tapes being broadcast were made a year or two before they were aired—that didn't make any difference. It didn't slow him down. He was certain I was sending signals to indicate who this woman was but was keeping back more detailed information.

In the beginning he merely talked to me about it. But talk soon turned into threats, which intensified as the weeks went by. Soon he began to threaten staff people. That's when we called the local law enforcement agency. "We'd like to do something about it," they told us, "but there's really nothing we can do until he actually does something." That's comforting, isn't it? By the time he acted, it might be too late! It was only when things got totally out of hand and he did act out that they were able to step in.

Your Almighty Protector

We live in a society in which we don't feel very safe or protected. We live in unsettling times.

That is why it comes as tremendously good news that when God is your Dad, you have an almighty protector. Because your Dad loves you, He protects you.

How does He do that? How can we believe God cares for His kids when we know there are people who have a relationship with Him who still suffer? Why is it that some people who enjoy a vibrant relationship with God still suffer unbelievable pain, even though they haven't done anything wrong to anybody? Can we really say God gives His kids any more protection than those who don't know Him? How does this protection work?

Psalm 91 describes how our perfect Dad protects His kids. In order to understand it, though, you've got to remember this: your Heavenly Father is not the same as your earthly father. Nor is He simply a bigger and better and stronger version of the same thing. Your Heavenly Father is the author and sustainer of life itself, the God of all creation. He explains most everything we need to know about His protection in this text:

> He who dwells in the secret place of the Most High shall abide under the shadow of the Almighty. I will say of the LORD, "He is my refuge and my fortress; My God, in Him I will trust."

> Surely He shall deliver you from the snare of the fowler and from the perilous pestilence. He shall cover you with His feathers, and under His wings you shall take refuge; His truth shall be your shield and buckler. You shall not be afraid of the terror by night, nor of the arrow that flies by day, nor of the pestilence that walks in darkness, nor of the destruction that lays waste at noonday.

> A thousand may fall at your side, and ten thousand at your right hand; but it shall not come near you. Only with your eyes shall you look, and see the reward of the wicked.

> Because you have made the LORD, who is my refuge, even the Most High, your habitation, no evil shall befall you, nor shall any plague come near your dwelling; For He shall give His angels charge over you, to keep you in all your ways. They shall bear you up in their hands, lest you dash your

foot against a stone. You shall tread upon the lion and the cobra, the young lion and the serpent you shall trample underfoot.

Because he has set his love upon Me, therefore I will deliver him; I will set him on high, because he has known My name. He shall call upon Me, and I will answer him; I will be with him in trouble; I will deliver him and honor him. With long life I will satisfy him, and show him My salvation (Psalm 91).

A Safe Living Environment

First, as His child, God offers you a totally safe living environment. You take up residence there as you yield your life to Him through Jesus Christ and as you begin to live according to His plan and His promises and His provision. It is critical that you understand this; it's the base upon which everything else rests.

The environment in which you find safety is spiritual in nature. It transcends the physical world in which you live day-in and day-out. It is a reality far greater than time and space. It is called *eternity*.

Christians sometimes casually refer to heaven as "the Sweet-By-and-By," the place they think they're going to live someday. But they don't understand how heaven and eternity are designed to impinge upon their existence *right now*. It's true that heaven and eternity won't fully shape us until that day when we will experience no suffering, no sorrow, no pain. In that day there will be no tears. In fact, you won't even have to worry about cholesterol!

But if you don't allow heaven and eternity to

affect the way you live right now, if you are hung up on earthly reality and your physical existence as the be-all and end-all of life, there's no way you'll ever feel safe. You are never going to feel secure. You will never feel protected.

Why not? There are simply too many everyday threats to your physical safety to permit a sense of protection. Disease, drunk drivers, thieves, natural disasters, accidents, financial cataclysms, divorce, unfair competition—our physical safety is always in peril. If you are hung up on physical safety as the only thing God can protect, you will always feel insecure. The fact is, even if you have a perfect physical existence—no disease, no struggles common to man, no accidents, no broken bones, no allergies, no anythings—and you are able to live an extraordinary long life (let's give you one hundred and ten years), even then your body will deteriorate. Even then you'll die.

What then? Whether you live forty years or one hundred and twenty years, sooner or later you'll have to deal with what comes next. And if you are hung up on physical existence, you will always struggle with feeling safe.

I assume you don't want to be saddled with such baggage. So how do you overcome these feelings? The psalmist has an answer for that. He says that as you enter into God's family through faith in His promises, you immediately set foot into eternity. Even when everything in your world collapses, you're safe. Time and space cannot touch the real you.

Paul talks about the same thing in the book of Colossians. In Colossians 3:3-4, the apostle says of those who are in Christ, "For you died, and your life is hidden with Christ in God. When Christ who is our life appears, then you also will appear with Him in glory." When your life is hidden in Christ, you are totally safe.

Some people who look at the apostle Paul can't figure out why he was able to do what he did. They can't imagine how he lived with such reckless abandon. How could he say things like, "For me to live is Christ, and to die is gain"?

I'll tell you why he was able to do that. It was because he had entered into an eternal relationship with God. He knew that whether he lived or died, he belonged to the Lord. The Lord was going to take care of him. Because the Lord had everything in control, even the difficulties in Paul's life could be handled. God could have stopped them at any moment—Paul knew that. But Paul trusted that God had a place prepared for him forever.

That's how he could throw himself recklessly into life, determined to give himself to God every day that God granted him. He loved serving the Lord. He wasn't interested in living just for himself. He knew that if he were healed, it was not just to say, "Boy, I feel great today!" He knew the whole reason for his existence was to proclaim the good news of new life in Jesus Christ. God would protect him. How? By giving him the knowledge of an eternity to come with Christ.

Nobody and *nothing* can take from you your relationship with God through Jesus Christ. That's Paul's passionate message in the book of Romans. "I am persuaded," Paul wrote, "that neither death nor life, nor angels nor principalities nor powers, nor things present nor things to come . . . can separate you from the love of God which is in Christ Jesus" (*see* Romans 8:38).

Jesus Himself says that when you enter into a personal relationship with God, you are in the palm of His hand. He will allow nothing to snatch you out of a relationship with Him (*see* John 10:28-29). He will protect you forever. He has an abiding place, a dwelling place for you with Him forever. As you dwell in the secret place of the Most High, you live in an environment that is completely safe. You will be "abiding under the shadow of the Almighty." What a wonderful promise that is!

Bruin Theology

Several years ago a fascinating nature film came out called *The Bear.* It told the story of a little Kodiak bear cub whose mother died. Trying to survive, the cub went nosing around for something to eat. Suddenly it stumbled upon a huge, full-grown male Kodiak bear who reared up to a terrifying height of eighteen feet.

The cub thought he was lunch meat. End of story. Kaput. But he was wrong. In fact, the two bears become fast friends. The rest of the film details the adventures of this little bear with his friend the big bear. They have lots of fun together.

At one point the bears are separated. The cub is on his own and tries like mad to find the big bear, but he can't. One day while roaming in the meadow, he's spotted by a huge, full-grown, extremely powerful and hungry mountain lion. The cub looks like easy pickings. So the big cat begins to stalk the cub, shadowing him from a distance. Finally, the time is perfect. The little bear is moving toward a cliff from which there is no escape. At just the right moment, the mountain lion streaks toward the cub as fast as he can. The cub sees what's happening and starts running furiously away—until he reaches the cliff.

He's trapped. Below the cliff foams a raging river. The cub's only option is to climb onto a tree root that's sticking out from the bank. He crawls out backward, edging away from the snarling and clawing mountain lion. Suddenly the cub loses his grip and plunges into the river.

Not to worry. He bobs up and finds himself surfing on a floating log. Great scenery!

He doesn't know it, but he's not out of danger yet. The mountain lion quickly sizes up the situation and realizes that, sooner or later, the river is going to get shallow. Then he'll dine on cub meat. He takes off, bounding powerfully and gracefully away. He continues to run until he finds what he was looking for. The cub has fallen off the log in shallow water. His protection is gone.

The end looks near. There they are—just the cub and the mountain lion. The big cat moves in for the kill, swipes at the bear, and scratches him. The bear begins to bleed.

The cub knows this is it. His chips are about to be cashed in. The only thing left to do is what he has seen his friend, the big bear, do. He rears back on his haunches, stands on his back legs—he's now all of four feet tall—and roars. Sort of.

The mountain lion looks at him as if to say, "You've got to be kidding."

"Roar," the cub says again.

Suddenly, the cougar pauses and seems to take note. Could there really be a giant inside this little bear? "Roar," the cub speaks again. The mountain lion starts backing up. Now the little bear cub is feeling good. "Roar," he says once more. The mountain lion backpedals even quicker.

But not because of the cub. Unbeknownst to the little bear, the big bear is standing right behind him, all eighteen menacing feet extended. He's moving threateningly toward that mountain lion. And the cat wants nothing to do with him.

Do you get the picture? That little bear cub is standing in the shadow of an unbelievably powerful creature—a creature who has the cub's best interests at heart and who has the means to protect him. That's the picture the psalmist has in mind: "He who dwells in the secret place of the Most High shall abide under the shadow of the Almighty."

You don't know what a growl is until you've heard the Lord's.

Protection from Temptation

Your perfect Dad's protection touches every area of your life. But it extends way beyond that. It protects you, he says, "From the snare of the fowler"—that is, from anything that would tempt you to wander away from the life God has for you.

Let's be honest. There are all kinds of things that would lure us away from the protection of the Lord. The enemy consistently tries to convince us to do those things that would take us outside of God's plan.

But our Dad loves us so much that, even in the midst of those temptations, He provides a way of escape (*see* 1 Corinthians 10:13). The problem comes when we don't take advantage of His route of escape.

The protection is there as we dwell in Him, but we're sitting ducks when we choose not to dwell in

Him. When we choose to move outside of His protection, we get clobbered.

Just last week I was talking with a young woman who had gotten herself into horrible debt due to her robust use of credit cards. By her own admission, if she had them, she'd use them—regardless of the difficulties they caused.

I suggested that God had given her the means of escape from her temptation. In this case, it took the form of a pair of scissors. All she needed to do was pick up those scissors, cut her cards into incredibly small, hopelessly unmatchable pieces, and she would be able to handle the temptation that was wrecking havoc in her life.

She mulled this novel idea over and then replied, "I would do that, but I just might need them in a pinch. Besides, clerks sometimes ask for them as additional identification."

Zoom! There went her route of escape. I suspect she's got some pretty tough times ahead of her.

How easy it is at such times to blame God! As we lick our wounds we say to Him, "Well, where were You when I needed You? How come You allowed this thing to happen? I don't care if I was doing something I shouldn't have been doing—You still should have been there on my behalf."

When we say such things, we forget that God loves us so much He gives us freedom. He will protect us from the snare of the fowler . . . but we have to do our part. We must take the route of escape He provides and follow the directions He gives. The alternative is not too promising.

Pestilence, Be Gone!

The text also says He will protect us "from the perilous pestilence"—that is, from the ravages of disease.

Isn't it interesting that God often heals us of difficult physical conditions? He doesn't do it on command. He doesn't necessarily do it when we want Him to or as we want Him to. Nor does He necessarily do it all of the time. But many times, in response to our prayers, He does amazing works of healing. He reverses a diagnosis of terminal illness and releases us from the bondage of diseases that threaten to wipe us out.

Still, there are times when He chooses not to heal physically. But even in such cases, it's pretty much irrelevant. Remember, we are eternal beings. That is why Paul said in 1 Corinthians 15:19, "If in this life only we have hope in Christ, we are of all men the most pitiable." If this is it, if this world as we know it is the sum total of reality, our future is pretty bleak.

Thank God that this *isn't* it! Those whose lives are hidden in Christ are eternal. God has promised that no disease can ever keep us out of our eternal relationship with Him. Though the perilous pestilence may seem to touch our lives, He will provide His protection.

He will also be a covering for us. That's what the psalmist means when he talks about covering us with His feathers and resting under His wings. That's where we take refuge.

It's impossible to overestimate how important this is when you are hurting. How important it is to know that when you are up against it, you can run to the Lord and He will wrap you up in His arms and enfold you to Himself!

Truth Is Stronger than Spears

But His protection doesn't stop there. His truth will also protect you. "His truth shall be your shield and buckler." His truth, His Word, will provide a barrier for you against the assaults of the enemy. Naturally, this won't work if His truth is not in you. Nor will it work if you base your life on feelings or experiences. Many times your feelings are going to let you down. Many times the enemy will make you feel lousy about yourself, about life, about God, about everything.

God's truth is, He loves you anyway. Even if everybody else hates you. Even if everybody else rejects you. Even if everybody else thinks you are the biggest turkey on the face of the earth. God still says, "You are precious to Me."

His truth shall be for you a shield for protection, a "buckler," which was a small shield buckled around the forearm, able to be moved quickly. His shield will block the assaults of the enemy that would lie to you to destroy your sense of confidence and protection in the Lord.

As you exercise faith in Him, fear will no longer control you. "You shall not be afraid of the terror by night, nor of the arrow that flies by day," whether it's things that go bump in the night or reports of crime in the streets. Whatever it is, He will protect you from fear.

This very text was quoted in one of the most moving scenes of the 1951 film version of *A Christmas Carol*, generally recognized to be the finest screen adaptation of Dickens's story ever made. The ghost of Christmas yet-to-come has taken Ebenezer Scrooge to Bob Cratchet's household. Bob is late coming home from work and everyone seems strangely subdued. The lights are low and everyone is downcast. Mrs.

Cratchet is crying as "Master Peter" reads from the Good Book.

It's clear to everyone—except Scrooge—that Tiny Tim has died. The reason Bob is late is that he's out visiting his son's gravesite. Yet even in the family's deep sorrow, the words of Psalm 91 bring hope and strength. "You shall not be afraid of the terror by night, nor of the arrow that flies by day, nor of the pestilence that walks in darkness, nor of the destruction that lays waste at noonday. A thousand may fall at your side, and ten thousand at your right hand; but it shall not come near thee." Those were the words. And that's why, when Peter asks if he should stop reading, Mrs. Cratchet says no. She wants to hear more.

Like one man said, the opposite of fear is not courage. The opposite of fear is faith. When you have faith in the Lord and your trust is placed in the Lord, there is no need to be afraid. Your Dad has you in His hand, forever. Even when people all around you are falling apart or going to hell in a hand basket, your Dad will keep you safe.

No Evil Shall Befall You

The tenth verse of Psalm 91 promises that when you make God your dwelling place, when you hide your life in Christ, "no evil shall befall you, nor shall any plague come near your dwelling." A superficial reading of that verse prompts the response, "That's not true! Evil has befallen me. Look at this sickness in my child. Look at this struggle in my business. Look at this, that, and the other thing. What do you mean, no evil shall befall you?"

It's true this verse says, "No evil shall befall you." What does God mean?

As I burrowed into the text, I found something fascinating. Do you know what the word *befall* means? It means "to contort with anguish." It doesn't mean that evil won't come upon you. It says that evil won't double you up. Evil won't produce in you anxiety, because you know that despite the garbage, God has your life in control.

Jesus Himself said we're going to suffer tribulation. He told us we were going to have troubles and trials and struggles. That isn't the issue. The fact is, despite all that stuff, a person whose life is hidden in the Lord can't be wiped out.

Furthermore, He says, "No plague shall come near your dwelling." Now, how could that be true?

Well, where is your dwelling place? In the secret place of the Almighty! He's not simply talking about your physical existence. He's talking about your life in the Lord. The old person is gone, put to death and buried with Christ. You've been raised up to a brand new life, which is forever! Nothing can take that away from you. Nothing! Your Dad has said, "That plague stops right here. I have already defeated that in Jesus Christ—and My sons and daughters are safe with Me forever." Your Dad sends angels to enable you to keep following Him, to keep your way straight.

It's fascinating how Satan ripped this passage of Scripture out of context and gave just part of the picture. Do you remember when he was tempting Jesus to jump off the pinnacle of the temple? "Go ahead and do this," he urged, "because Scripture says, 'He shall give His angels charge over you.'" Then he cleverly skipped the next section and said, "They shall bear you up in their hands, lest you dash your foot against a stone." What was it that he conveniently forgot to quote? "He shall give His angels charge over you *to keep you in all your ways.*"

The whole purpose of ministering spirits is to enable God's people to live His life. It's not merely to protect you from physical difficulties or problems. They exist to encourage you to live in the fullness of the promises and the plans and the provisions of the Lord. Your perfect Dad doesn't want you to stub your toe in this world of sin.

Your Dad's Ironclad Promise

Your Dad protects you in every area of your life, now and forever. That is why the last part of Psalm 91 is so important. Listen to the clear promise that your Dad makes today. Understand what He's telling you.

In fact, why don't you insert your name into the text to personalize this promise and help you to remember that He's making you this offer today?

Because _____ has set his [her] love upon Me, therefore I will deliver_____ ; I will set _____ on high, because _____ has known My name. _____ shall call upon Me, and I will answer _____ ; I will be with_____ in trouble; I will deliver_____ and honor_____ . With long life I will satisfy , and show_____ My salvation.

Your Dad protects you, both now and forever. He invites you to hide your life in God through a personal relationship with Jesus Christ, yielding yourself to Him. Why not go after Him with everything you've got and let Him enfold you in His strong arms of love . . . forever?

Because your Dad loves you, He protects you.

CHAPTER SEVEN

My Dad Listens to Me

A young father admitted something to me the other day that I found both interesting and revealing. This guy has two beautiful little girls. One of them is three and the other is about six months. He struggles with being attentive to his three-year-old when she starts talking to him. Although he really desires to listen to her, a few seconds after she starts talking he is thinking about something else.

Now, don't get the wrong idea. He's a good dad. He's intentional about his relationship with his little girl and about helping her grow up so she can be everything God wants her to be. He loves her and shows her that love. Every day on his way home he thinks about what's going to transpire at the dinner table. He thinks through the kind of conversation he wants to have that evening and develops questions designed to get his daughter talking. He wants to be close to her and tie into the things that interest her.

Unfortunately, by the time his daughter understands the question, frames in her mind how she is going to respond, and finally spits it out, he's ten miles away. He's thinking about what happened at the office and what's going to be happening tomorrow; about a business deal he'll be making two or three weeks down the road; about house payments and dentist's bills and all kinds of other things. When suddenly he snaps back to reality and realizes that she's been chattering for minutes on end, he looks at her, smiles, and says, "That's really great, honey."

Now, she might have just said, "Daddy, I got stung by a bee today." She might have said, "I know I'm only three, but I'm moving out and living on my own next week." No matter. He always replies, "Oh, that's really great, honey."

His only consolation is knowing that she's so young she doesn't "get it" yet. She doesn't yet realize that he's not tuned in.

Or at least that was the illusion he lived under until a week or so ago. His little girl was talking to her mom and said, "You know Mommy, Daddy just is not a very good listener."

Three years old. Watch out!

The Shortage of Listening Ears

As a dad of three children, I would love to tell you that my friend is an exception to the rule. I would love to declare that most dads love to hear everything their kids have to say. I'd love to say that most dads can't wait for those precious moments in which their three-year-olds or four-year-olds or fifteen-year-olds bare their souls. I would love to tell you that most dads wait with bated breath for the wonderful things their kids will reveal to them. I'd love to tell you a lot of things, but that wouldn't make them true, would it?

The truth is, if there is anything that dads struggle with, it is listening to their kids.

David knows the problem. He told me this about childhood: "My dad worked, it seemed, almost all of the time. We really never talked much, and after dinner time, it was 'crash' on the sofa and watch a little TV." Chris likewise reported, "My dad never spoke to me or touched me except to reprimand me. He was a scary man, very overpowering and controlling." No listeners there!

And that is precisely why it's precious to know there is a Dad who faithfully listens to everything His kids say.

God sets the standard for what it is like to have a dad who listens, who takes seriously the thoughts and hurts of his kids. Your perfect Dad likes nothing more than to listen to His kids. He loves to spend personal time with each one of them. Not only does He have all the time in the world for His kids, but He longs to cultivate a relationship with each one of them based on their willingness to participate.

The funny thing is that when we look closely at God as a Dad, we find Him far more interested in listening to His kids than His kids are in listening and talking to Him.

Psalm 34 gives us a framework for understanding

how God listens to His kids. It not only explains how our perfect Dad manages this, but insists that anybody, right here and now, can have a Dad who listens to everything they say.

> The eyes of the LORD are on the righteous, and His ears are open to their cry. The face of the LORD is against those who do evil, to cut off the remembrance of them from the earth. The righteous cry out, and the LORD hears, and delivers them out of all their troubles. The LORD is near to those who have a broken heart, and saves such as have a contrite spirit [or those who are crushed in spirit]. Many are the afflictions of the righteous, but the LORD delivers him out of them all (Psalm 34:15-19).

God is committed to listening to His kids. He loves to hear from them. That's what David means when he says, "The eyes of the LORD are on the righteous, and His ears are open to their cry," and, "The righteous cry out, and the LORD hears, and delivers them out of all their troubles."

While I wish this were a comforting truth for most people, I'm afraid it's not. When some folks read these words, one particular word leaps out. *Righteous.* When they read that "the eyes of the Lord are on the *righteous* and His ears are open to their cry," and when they hear that the "*righteous* cry out and the Lord hears," they look at themselves and say, "Wait a minute! I guess that excludes me, because there is no way I am righteous. I'm not perfect. I don't see myself as holy—and if you were to ask my boss or my wife or my friends, they'd agree with me. Probably the last adjective they would use to describe me would be 'righteous.' So if God says in His Word that He's interested in listening to righteous people, I guess He's not interested in listening to me."

I've heard that kind of reasoning more times than I can count. The plain truth is, most of us don't see ourselves as righteous. Most of us can cite a million reasons why God probably wouldn't want to listen to us. We know we aren't everything that we should be (let alone what we could be), so why would God want to listen to people like us? If God listens only to the righteous, most of us appear to be left out.

Have you ever thought like that? I have, too. And that's the problem with taking verses out of their larger context. You come up with all kinds of unbiblical ideas.

When you place these statements into the context of the whole of the Bible, something very different emerges. So maybe that's what we should take some time to do—look at the larger context. Then you'll begin to see that these verses contain some powerfully good news.

A Text without a Context Is a Pretext

The apostle Paul states clearly that no one, on his own, is righteous. Romans 3:10 maintains that "there is none righteous, no, not one." In verse 23 of that same chapter he says, "For all have sinned and fall short of the glory of God."

Am I cheering you up yet?

John expresses this even more graphically in his first epistle: "If we say that we have no sin, we deceive ourselves, and the truth is not in us. . . . If we say that we have not sinned, we make Him a liar, and His word is not in us" (1 John 1:8,10).

Both of these men echo what Isaiah said many centuries before. He told his own people, "All our righteousness is as filthy rags." Before the Lord, every fabulous thing we think we do looks like trash.

Unless I miss my guess, as you review your life, you *shouldn't* conclude you are a terribly righteous person. It may be because of things you have done. It may be because of things you have said. Perhaps it's because you have oriented your entire life against God and His best for you. I don't know. But I'm pretty sure you are not a person who sees himself as being righteous. Nor should you.

The truth is, everybody is in exactly the same boat. No matter how they might look or feel, on his own, nobody is perfect. Nobody is righteous. Nobody is holy, clean, or pure.

That's why it comes as such fantastic news to hear the rest of what God says in His Word. For He says He gives you His righteousness when you acknowledge Jesus as Savior. The very righteousness of Jesus Christ becomes yours.

Paul talks about this in Romans 4:24-25. He says the righteousness of Jesus Christ "shall be imputed to us who believe in Him who raised up Jesus our Lord from the dead, who was delivered up because of our offenses, and was raised because of our justification." Or as he writes in 2 Corinthians 5:21, "For He made Him who knew no sin to be sin for us, that we might become the righteousness of God in Him."

When you enter into a personal relationship with God by believing in Jesus Christ and God becomes your Dad, He covers you with the righteousness of Jesus Himself. He washes you with the blood of Jesus.

He cleanses you so that whatever has been is no longer. From then on, He sees you not as you were but in the purity of Jesus Christ.

And that, my friend, is *righteous!*

Those who belong to Christ get heard. When you cry out, He listens. Not because of anything you have done or been, but because of who He is and what He has done for you. He has welcomed you into His family. He has made you one of His own. He has cleansed you in the blood of Jesus Christ. He now perceives you as—ready for this?—*perfectly* righteous.

That's why the words of David apply to you—*the eyes of the Lord are on you, and His ears are open to your cry.* When you cry out, the Lord hears and He delivers you out of all of your troubles.

Fantastic! Because of what God has done through Jesus Christ, you have a Dad who will listen to you anytime, all of the time, about anything you can name.

Kinks in the Phone Lines

Before we go any further, let me remind you of one potential problem area. While through Jesus Christ you have a Dad who listens to you, it's possible for you to hinder the process. Decisions you make and attitudes you express can and do obstruct the flow of communication between God and you.

Scripture describes a variety of these hindrances. Peter, for example, tells husbands that failure to honor their wives and live with them in an understanding way will hinder their prayers. That's a pretty ominous statement, isn't it? If you don't "honor" your wife—if you don't value her, prize her, or count her as precious—neither will God "honor" your prayers.

You might as well save your breath. Likewise, if you make no attempt to understand your wife, caring little about what she thinks or how she feels, God will disregard your requests. Failure in this area will block communication between you and your Dad.

Psalm 66:18 details another hindrance to open communication. It says, "If I regard iniquity in my heart, the Lord will not hear." If you dwell on things that God condemns, if you allow your mind to be captivated by that which takes you away from God, if you allow yourself to be caught up in idolatrous and wicked things, things that are dead set against God's desires for your life, you will block communication with the Lord.

That's not because the Lord wants it this way. In this instance, the problem isn't Him; it's you. The more time you allow yourself to mull over in your mind things that are ungodly and the less time you think about God, the more distant you become from Him. The more distant the relationship, the less communication that exists. And suddenly, you'll find yourself in a jam and call out to Him. Don't be surprised if He says, "It seems to Me I've heard that voice before. But then, maybe I'm mistaken. It's been such a long time since I heard it!"

You and I must recognize that we can do things to block communication with our Dad. That is why God has provided the means to clear away the debris and reopen clear channels. First John 1:9 says, "If we confess our sins, He is faithful and just to forgive us our sins and to cleanse us from all unrighteousness." If along the way you slip into patterns that take you away from God, He gives you the opportunity to get right again. Simply by admitting your sin and desiring to turn from those ways, the line is open once again.

Your relationship with God through Jesus Christ cleanses you and allows God to listen to everything you have to say. The lines of communication are wide open. You can speak and your Dad will listen.

Help In Troubled Times

At all times, God loves to hear from His kids. Scripture tells us, for example, that He inhabits the praises of His people. He loves to listen to His kids praise Him, worship Him, and honor Him with their lips. He relishes those opportunities. We also know that whenever two or more of His kids hang out together, He is right in the middle of their conversation. He loves it when they say things to build up each other. He's ecstatic when they speak in ways that help one another to live more fully for Him.

But we know He especially listens to them when they are in trouble. He is extremely sensitive to His kids when they hurt, when they're filled with heartache, anguish, or distress.

Parents, isn't it true that whenever your little tykes cried out, you instantly paid attention? If you left your child in a nursery filled with a herd of kids where the din was so loud you could hardly hear yourself think, and you were a hundred feet away when your child cried out, I'll bet you heard only that one little voice. Your first desire would be to rush in and bring comfort. "It's okay honey, Daddy is here, Mommy is here. I'm going to help you now. It's going to be okay." Or when you took that little one to the doctor's office for an immunization and the nurse took your child and they disappeared behind the door. Suddenly, you hear "Whaaaaa!" What do you want to do? You want to burst through the door and promise that child an ice cream cone, a pony ride, a Cinnabon. Something! Anything! "Don't cry!" Isn't that true?

That's a picture of how much your heavenly Father desires to hear you when you hurt. How earnestly He listens when you cry out, when you are down, when you feel as though you can't make sense out of life! His ears are wide open to His kids' cries. "The eyes of the LORD are on the righteous, and His ears are open to their cry. . . . The righteous cry out, and the LORD hears, and delivers them out of all their troubles."

Please understand God never plays favorites. It doesn't make any difference if you are powerful or popular or wealthy or have some wonderful position in society. All He cares about is that you are willing to cry out to Him, to communicate with Him when you hurt.

The Bible gives us some beautiful examples of people who were willing to do that. I think of David, who time and again cried out to his Dad when he was in trouble. When he was in the pits of despair, even when he was hurting because of his own sin, David cried out to his Dad. He knew his Dad was the only one who could care for him. He knew that as he cried out to his Dad, his Dad would care for him. He would be right there for him, listening to everything that was in his heart, eager to respond and meet his need.

The same thing was true for Jesus. Often He withdrew from the crowds to talk to His Dad. After long, grueling days and nights ministering to the needs of others until there was nothing left in Him, He'd spend the whole night talking to His Dad. He could have gone home and sacked out and told His friends He was suffering from burnout and probably wouldn't be in the next day, but He didn't. He prayed. In the deepest, darkest moments of His life, Jesus talked to His Dad. He cried out to His Dad because He knew His Dad would listen and bear Him up in His arms.

If you want your Dad to listen to you, take a lesson from these two men. Cry out to Him in your time of struggle. If you give verbal assent to the possibility of talking to God, especially when you are struggling, but you never do it, that's not worth much, is it? The only time you demonstrate your belief is when you build it into the fabric of your everyday life.

That's why Paul could say it was important for God's people to pray without ceasing. His students didn't have to think, *Oh my goodness, what am I going to do now? Wait! I'd better pray.* Their relationship with their Dad was so tight that prayer would be an automatic response. They knew without question that their Dad heard them when they cried out.

Heaven's Delivery Service

It's great that your Dad hears the cries of your heart, but what if He couldn't do anything about it? What if He was impotent to help?

Of course, that's not a problem with your Dad! When He hears, He responds—and things happen. "The righteous cry out, and the LORD hears, and delivers them out of all of their troubles. The LORD is near to those who have a broken heart, and saves such as have a contrite spirit. Many are the afflictions of the righteous, but the LORD delivers him out of them all."

The Lord delivers His people. He responds in His time and in His way; but when you cry out, He will respond. Mark it down.

117

Many of us struggle with this. We don't like it that God responds in His time and in His way. We'd much rather He would respond in our time and in our way. Often we even go so far as to give Him a timetable which we think He must keep. We'll say things like, "Lord, I need this house to be sold by the end of March. That gives you two full weeks!" Then, if the house doesn't sell on our timetable, we immediately assume that He didn't care enough to listen to us. Either He didn't hear us, or if He did, He wasn't concerned enough to do anything about it. As a result, we sometimes even go so far as to question our faith. All because He didn't function in accordance with our time schedule!

It'd be so much easier for us if we'd learn from people like David and Jesus. Consider Psalm 40:1-2. What a wonderful statement of the heart of someone who *got it!* "I waited patiently for the LORD," he says. He gave Him twenty-three minutes? No! "I waited patiently for the LORD; and He inclined to me, and heard my cry. He also brought me up out of a horrible pit, out of the miry clay, and set my feet upon a rock, and established my steps."

The key word here is *patiently*. He waited. "I waited patiently for the LORD." That is, "I believed somehow if I brought to Him my need, He would respond in a way that would be best for me. And I believed He had a better handle on that than I did, so I trusted Him!"

Look at Jesus in the garden. He knows that in a few minutes He is going to be arrested and then crucified. As He was praying, Matthew tells us that His sweat became as drops of blood. "Oh My Father," He prayed, "if it is possible, let this cup pass from Me; nevertheless, not as I will, but as You will." Even in the darkest moment of His life, Jesus knew that God would respond to Him—but He allowed God to respond in His time and in His way. Why? Because He was living a life submitted to His Dad.

That's the key to communicating with your Dad and having Him listen and respond. Submit your life to Him in joyful devotion.

Broken Hearts Welcome Here

God listens to all His kids, but the Lord is especially near to those who have a broken heart, according to Psalm 34. He saves those who are crushed in spirit. That means He is exceedingly sensitive to you when you are struggling and admit you're struggling. But it also means He is especially sensitive when you are open to Him to allow Him to respond in the way that He chooses.

Paul demonstrated how to do this. He reports in 2 Corinthians 12 that there was a time in his life when he was really up against it. We don't know for sure whether he had some kind of physical malady—theories range from epilepsy to malaria to a significant eye disease—or if he was alluding to all the hassles he faced day in and day out. Whatever it was, it was a tremendous and pressing difficulty.

Three times he took his problem to God and three times it appeared as though God wasn't interested in meeting his needs. Finally the Lord spoke to him and said, "My grace is sufficient for you, for My strength is made perfect in weakness." Paul had to trust his Dad on this one. In fact, through this incident, Paul learned to trust God more deeply than he ever had. I believe it was a pivotal experience in Paul's life. It helped him understand how much his Dad really loved him and what his Dad intended to do through his life.

Years later his perfect Dad would ask Paul to go to Rome to be a witness for Him. Paul was told that it was going to cost him. The apostle knew he was in for big trouble. He was going to be jailed. He was going to be beaten. He was shipwrecked on the way and a venomous snake fastened onto his arm. God told him these kinds of things were going to happen.

Twice Paul could have extricated himself from the whole mess. In Acts 25 we are told that Felix tried to get Paul to bribe him. For two whole years he waited, hoping that Paul would crease his palm with a few shekels. But Paul never did, because he knew God wanted him in Rome. Later, after Paul defended himself before King Agrippa, the king said, "You know the guy's not guilty. Let's get serious here. And if he hadn't appealed to Rome I would just cut him loose."

Paul knew what Agrippa was suggesting. The apostle was not exactly one eggroll short of a combination plate. This guy was sharp. He knew Agrippa expected him to say, "Oh, wait, wait! I'm gonna retract this whole plea here. No big deal. Let's pretend it didn't happen and I'll just walk. Then we'll go back to business as usual." It could have happened, but it didn't. Why? Because Paul had submitted his life to his Dad. He cried out to Him with his life, he put his life in His Dad's hands and he was willing to allow his Dad to shape him and direct him in the way that he should go.

God loves to hear from His kids. He responds to them especially when they cry out. He listens to them and responds in a way designed to build them up to be everything they were meant to be. He wants them to experience His joy to the fullest measure.

Is This Your Confidence?

Do you have such a confidence? Are you convinced that your perfect Dad is just waiting to hear from you, that He longs to spend time with you? If you don't enjoy such confidence, you can.

John says it so well in 1 John 5:14: "Now this is the confidence that we [you] have in Him, that if we [you] ask anything according to His will, He hears us [you]. And if we [you] know that He hears us [you], whatever we [you] ask, we [you] know that we [you] have the petitions that we [you] have asked of Him."

Read once again the truth about your Dad. And begin to live in the reality of that truth:

The eyes of the LORD are on the righteous, and His ears are open to their cry.

The righteous cry out, and the LORD hears, and delivers them out of all their troubles. The LORD is near to those who have a broken heart, and saves such as have a contrite spirit. Many are the afflictions of the righteous, but the LORD delivers him out of them all (Psalm 34:15,17-19).

God loves to listen to you when you open your heart to Him. Make it your aim to spend time with Him today. Tell Him your hurts. Share with Him your joys. Bring Him your requests. He's waiting to hear from you right now. Why not allow Him to respond to you in the fullness of His love? And never, ever forget:

Because your Dad loves you, He listens to you.

CHAPTER EIGHT

My Dad
Builds Me Up

Chris was adopted. Unlike some adopted kids who see themselves as rejects, she thinks of herself as especially chosen. And she's convinced she had the greatest mom and dad on the face of the earth.

Chris positively glows when she describes her dad. Much of that radiance shows through even when she writes about him:

> When I was in elementary school in seventh grade, I failed miserably. I tried so hard to get good grades. My dad was always there to help me with my homework. He knew I could do the work and took every opportunity to build up my self-esteem.

> In seventh grade, my dad took off time from

work, often to meet with teachers and other school staff members who wanted me tested for special education. But Dad knew better. He fought them all the way.

He found a parochial school for my eighth and ninth grade years. The first term I was on the "B" honor role. Dad worked with me for four or more hours most nights after school. I went on to graduate from high school and from college with a "B" average. I credit my dad for having believed in me and for helping me to strive to do my best.

Chris's dad exemplified what I believe is one of *the* most important functions of being a dad. He worked to build her up. He saw in her what she could not see in herself. He gave himself to her to shore up her weaknesses and to expand her areas of strength. When she thought she had nothing left, he moved in and gave her his strength to lean on. He helped her become more than she thought she could be, and in the process he developed within her an inner strength to meet the demands of her present and move with confidence into the future.

Would that all dads functioned like Chris's dad! Regrettably, they don't.

Bookstore shelves and letters in my personal files are filled with stories of people whose dads couldn't care less about their kids. Dads who filled their lives with everything but their sons and daughters. Dads who spent most of their time working, fishing, hunting, golfing, fiddling with their old car, working on their latest building project, or going out with friends to the local tavern. Whatever precious time these dads had, it wasn't reserved for their kids.

Ted's dad fit this mold. He told me that his father "was always gone hunting and fishing during his spare time with his brothers or cousins." Denise, too, confessed she had no relationship with her dad because he "did a lot of running around and drinking." Lew's comments were the most poignant of all: "Dad never attended any sporting event I was in. I suppose he was at my graduation, but I don't recall him being there. He was a hunter and fisherman deluxe."

Maybe such dads grew up themselves without a father as a role model. I don't know. But for whatever reason, they're clueless about how to build up their kids. They don't know what to do. So instead of trying, they opt out—and leave their kids to flounder.

It's possible you see your own childhood in those comments. You may feel where you've ended up today is a function of default rather than design. You may admit that you have had to make your own way through life, that you have never had any significant person to point the right way. You may have felt overwhelmed by weakness, as though you were unable to meet the challenges. You had nobody to turn to. When you hit the deck, you weren't able to get up.

As a result, you find yourself in an uncomfortable position. Now you're the one who's supposed to be building up your kids . . . and you don't have the foggiest notion of what to do. So you do what comes naturally—nothing. You, too, are opting out. You don't know where to find the instruction manual titled *How to Build Up Your Kids.*

Not Just the Book, But the Author

Well, catch this! Because your Dad loves you, He is committed to doing whatever it takes to build you up. He sees in you what you can't see in yourself. He knows all about the strengths, abilities, and talents that He has placed deep within you. He is committed to helping you discover them yourself and to develop them so you might put them to work. Along the way, He meets you at your points of weakness and gives you His strength. Not only are you never alone, but you have available to you a reservoir of power that comes from on high—power that dwarfs anything you could hope to obtain on your own.

If you'd like to discover how this works, I suggest you join me in looking at the story of a man named Gideon. As you follow the most significant episodes in Gideon's life, you will see how the heavenly Father works to build up His kids. Much more than that, you will find a fantastic role model to follow. If you were to integrate your heavenly Dad's habits into your own life, you'd quickly see an incredible difference in the lives of your kids.

A New View of You

The first thing Gideon teaches us is that our heavenly Father builds us up by giving us a whole new view of ourselves. That's how the story of Gideon begins.

The sixth chapter of Judges describes a young man who sees himself as a loser from a community of losers. The Israelites were on the bottom. Though they had been a strong and proud people, their strength had dissipated. The further away they moved from their relationship with God, the less strength and ability they enjoyed. By Gideon's time they were living far from God. The result: foreigners unmercifully attacked them.

The Midianites were one of these marauding groups. Each year they swept down to terrorize the helpless Israelites. They waited until the Hebrews had planted and grown their crops and were ready to harvest. Then they'd invade like a swarm of locusts, destroying everything in their path. Crops, sheep, oxen, donkeys, homes, vineyards—they ravaged everything. No wonder the Israelites became paranoid, scared of their own shadows.

Such a scenario helps to explain Gideon's location when God came to greet him. The Lord found him hiding in a wine press.

Gideon was in that wine press to avoid the Midianites. But he wasn't making wine. He was threshing wheat!

How would you greet such a man? Would you address him as a loser? God didn't. Instead, this is what he said: "The LORD is with you, you mighty man of valor! . . . Go in this might of yours, and you shall save Israel from the hand of the Midianites. Have I not sent you?" (Judges 6:12,14).

It doesn't take a molecular biologist to realize that somebody had a wrong perception of this young man. Either:

1. God had the wrong address and was talking to the wrong guy (sort of like when the police knock down the door of the wrong house in a drug bust); or

2. God was a couple of sandwiches short of a picnic; or

3. God so desired that His people whip the Midianites that He would grasp at anything—and it just happened that Gideon was the graspee; or

4. God was filled with a fantasy about what this young man would be able to accomplish; or

5. Just maybe, God saw in Gideon something that nobody else, including Gideon himself, was able to see.

As you follow the story it becomes clear that the last option is the right choice.

God used this greeting to begin opening Gideon's mind to an entirely new perception of himself. God wasn't concerned about Gideon's own warped self-perception. He wanted to replace that view with a brand new vision—a totally different understanding and perspective on his life and what he would do.

It's my experience that God works to build up all His kids in exactly this manner. It was certainly true in my own life.

If you had asked me in high school what I was going to do with my life, becoming a pastor would not have appeared on my list. It never entered my mind. Early in high school I decided to become a newspaper reporter and immersed myself in journalism. As I got older I decided to be an attorney. I thought there was all kinds of action in the law. But never did I think about the pastorate. I just wasn't a church person. I didn't have a personal relationship with Jesus Christ. Why on earth would I have any zeal for God or things religious?

But literally minutes after coming into a personal relationship with Jesus Christ as a seventeen-year-old senior, I knew what I would do with my life. God gave me a whole new view of myself. In some mysterious way that I can't fully describe, He let me know

He wanted me to teach His people. He wanted me to encourage His people as a pastor. He didn't care about any religious gaps in my background or about any of my shortcomings in character. He simply communicated to me that there was a whole lot more for me and that all He wanted me to do was trust Him and walk with Him. I didn't have to worry about the huge gaps in my life; that was His job.

Across the years, I have seen Him work in the lives of others in the same way. He rearranges their thinking and redirects their lives. While earthly fathers can be extremely helpful in this process, nonetheless nobody can give you as full a view of who you were designed to be as your heavenly Father. God sees more for you than you can begin to see for yourself. He sees more for you than anybody else could, too. God isn't trapped by your past. He sees you in the light of what He has designed you to be and begins the process of building you up by giving you a new perception of yourself.

You might not have a very positive view of yourself. Maybe you had a real struggle growing up. Perhaps childhood traumas derailed your development. For years you have wallowed in self-pity, and the only self-description that seems to fit is a "dysfunctional, co-dependent of an adult child survivor." It's possible that you don't see a bright future ahead.

Your perfect Dad wants to push all of that out of the way and replace it with a brand new view of you. He shows you that you are His child and that He gives you all kinds of strengths and abilities and talents. He tells you He has a significant place laid out for you and helps you to understand that He is going to use you in a special way in His family.

You must come to believe this. You will never be all you were meant to be apart from adopting God's view of you. But when you enter into a relationship with God as your Dad and you let Him begin to replace your defective self-view with His understanding of you, all bets are off. Things really begin to change.

God's Exercise Program

Gideon's life also teaches us that your Dad continues to build you up by walking you through faith-building experiences. He gave Gideon several opportunities to build his strength and his faith.

Once He instructed Gideon to tear down the altar of Baal that his father Joash had constructed. On that very site Gideon was to construct a new altar dedicated to God. Then he was told to take a bull from his father's herd and offer it up to God as a sacrifice.

Gideon was no dummy. He understood what would happen to him if he carried out God's orders. He knew that although his people were supposed to be committed to God, they weren't. Over the years they had allowed their faith in God to become diluted until they began to worship Baal, a false god. So if Gideon were to go up and obliterate this altar that had become so central to the community, the townspeople would be after his hide.

But God urged him on. "You can do this, man! Go in and rip the thing down, then build Me a new one. Offer a bull on it. It will be great." *I bet it will,* Gideon must have thought. But Gideon did what he was asked to . . . at night. He didn't boldly saunter in at high noon and announce, "All right cowboys, watch this." He sneaked in after dark with his friends and dismantled the shrine. Quietly. Then he built a new one.

130

("Quiet with the nails, fellas!") He erected the altar, sacrificed the bull on it, high-tailed it out of there, and thought he had done what he was supposed to do. Everything was just great.

Until the morning newspapers hit the streets. The next day the local populace was enraged. They sent their best investigative reporters to find out who would dare do such a thing. Finally it came down to Gideon, the young son of Joash. They stormed the old man's place and said to Joash, "You send out your son that we might kill him." Somehow, I'm not sure where, Joash got up the nerve to stand up for his son and for God. He said, "I'll tell you what. If Baal really is a god, then let him stand up for himself. If he really is a god, let him take out Gideon. Let's just do it that way." Surprisingly, the people bought it and backed off. And nothing happened to Gideon.

That day Gideon's faith in God and his resolve to live for Him took a giant step forward.

Did I say a giant step forward? Well, that's right, but He still had a long way to go. I figure that giant step forward only got him halfway to first base. Still, he was on the right track, which is probably why God came to Gideon a little later and asked him to lead God's people against the Midianites. Now remember, Gideon's only halfway to first base. That explains why he asks the Lord for a sign. Had he made it safely to first he wouldn't have needed a sign. (I realize this might not be good baseball, but it's good theology.)

So Gideon asked God for a sign. If I had been God, I probably would have responded, "Oh, brother. You must not be the man for the job. If what we pulled off already wasn't enough for you, this isn't going to work." But that isn't the way the Lord operates. Gideon needed a sign, so God gave him a sign. He met him exactly at his point of weakness, and again Gideon's faith and resolve and strength to live for God took a giant step forward.

Had you asked Gideon at the time if he realized what God was doing in his life, if he knew his Dad was building into him strength and character, he would have looked at you cross-eyed. But as we study Gideon's life from our vantage point, we realize that's exactly what God was doing.

So now Gideon's on first base. Great! But if the object is to score, he's still got some base running to do. So God asks Gideon to assemble an army to attack the Midianites. Gideon (who after all is on first base) thought that was okay. He drafted all of the people and ended up with thirty-two thousand men. He wasn't fully comfortable with that number against the hordes of Midian, but at least it was start.

God thought it was a good number to start with, too, but His idea of improving it was unique. It was as if he looked at Gideon's team, saw it stocked with a bullpen of five relief pitchers, and shouted, "What? Five relievers? That's not good enough, not for my team. I'll tell you what we're going to do. Get rid of four of them. Or better yet, fire the whole crew. This team don't need no relievers."

Gideon obeyed and pared the troops from 32,000 to 22,000 and finally to 300. Understand that this ragtag group was to take on an army described "as numerous as locusts; and their camels were without number, as the sand by the seashore in multitude." It looked like the Cincinnati Reds were about to take on the Converse Elementary School B Team.

Why did God insist on such an arrangement? He wanted Gideon to see that he could never pull off this operation on his own. If he were to succeed, he had to rely upon his Dad's strength. God knew that if there were 32,000 or even 22,000 Israelite troops, they would begin to gloat and say, "Look what we were able to pull off. Look how great we are!" But with 300? No chance!

God also wanted Gideon to learn that as he trusted Him and stepped out in faith, He would do some radically unique things in his life. But it would never happen unless Gideon had a significant challenge staring him in the face.

What's Good for Gideon Is Good for the Gander

Do you know there's no way your Dad can build strength in you apart from these faith-building experiences? I have had so many of them I can't begin to count them. And I have to be honest—I have not enjoyed any of them. Not one. Faith-building experiences stretch you in ways you are convinced you cannot be stretched. They're painful. They're difficult. They call for what you believe you do not have.

Early in my relationship with the Lord I had what I thought were some monumental faith-building experiences. But they dim in comparison to things I have experienced since. In the beginning, they were little things, like trusting God for my tuition to go through college. Across the years, these experiences escalated to include challenges like significant physical problems in my family or trying to start a church from scratch. At every juncture it was incredibly difficult for me to trust God. But as I trusted Him, He built my strength, my resolve, my faith in Him.

When we began Crossroads Church and I realized what some of the up-front costs were going to be—everything from renting an office to installing a telephone to renting worship space to securing sound equipment and microphones and curriculum materials and on and on—I was overwhelmed. One day in prayer, I said to the Lord, "You know, God, I would be much more comfortable if we had about six thousand bucks in the bank." Then in the whirlwind of activity that surrounded putting together our first Sunday worship service I forgot about the prayer. By the end of the week when the offerings had come in and the gifts had been tabulated and we had paid all our bills, I looked at our checkbook. We had six thousand and twenty-five dollars in the bank. It was as if God were saying to me, "Son, this really isn't necessary, but I will see your six thousand and raise you twenty-five." I saw my own faith, resolve, and strength in God take a giant step forward.

(The funny thing is, we didn't even have to use this money until several years later when we purchased property for a building!)

As your Dad takes you through these faith-building experiences, you can expect a couple of things to happen. On the one hand, He is going to call forth every amount of personal strength and ability you have. He is going to call you to put everything you have on the line; to invest everything you are in His life.

Some people seem to think that a relationship with God is like being a hand puppet. They just stand there and wait for Him to move His hand in and jostle them around. They don't see why they should invest anything in the process.

But the lives of vibrant Christians throughout the ages testify that until you invest everything you have and everything you are in your relationship with God, nothing significant is going to happen. He wants to enter into a dynamic partnership with you.

On the other hand, God will more than match your strength as He pours His strength into your life. The truth is, apart from Him, you could never do what He has in mind for you.

Immediately before He ascended into heaven, Jesus told His disciples to go and wait in Jerusalem for the provision of the Holy Spirit. "But you shall receive power when the Holy Spirit has come upon you; and you shall be witnesses to Me in Jerusalem, and in all Judea and Samaria, and to the end of the earth" (Acts 1:8). In other words, "I'm not asking you to do this thing on your own. I'm going to give you unbelievable strength. You've got to trust Me on this one. But when I infuse you with My strength, understand that I'm doing it so that you might become effective for Me."

So they went and waited . . . and God poured into their lives something they had never before experienced. When you study the early church and see the amazing things that were accomplished through these people, you realize it was because they invested everything they had in God, and then God plugged in His strength and the whole thing took off.

God never expected that His people could live His life apart from His power. Part of building you up in His life is helping you to rely on His power. You must assume that He will express His strength at your points of weakness, that He will bring His power to bear on your life in such a way that you will do outrageous

135

things for Him. He'll do this through countless faith-building experiences and He'll walk with you, stand beside you, and strengthen you through them all.

Gideon's Final Lesson

As you trust Him to do so, your perfect Dad will accomplish His purposes in your life. He will build you up. He will use you. He will expand His kingdom through you. That's what Gideon learned.

Consider what God brought about through the life of this young man. Under his leadership, God destroyed an enemy that was so great it couldn't be counted. Gideon's three hundred men didn't just back them off; they ran them out of the country. They utterly destroyed those who would oppose God and His people. The Lord built strength and resolve in Gideon by calling upon his human strength, then by adding to it His own. All along the way He brought honor and respect to His glorious name.

It amazes me to think that God is committed to doing exactly this for all of His kids. It's far too easy to see yourself as not worth very much—as a person who isn't special or unique or who doesn't have anything God would want to use for His purposes. Indeed, if you had a dad like Toni's, it's easy to understand why you could feel this way. "My father's academic and career achievements are outstanding," she told me, "and I've never felt that mine were acceptable. The older I have become, the more often he points out my shortcomings." With that kind of "encouragement," I can understand why you might believe you have nothing special to offer.

But the truth is, as you trust God as your Dad, He will build you up. He will use you in His service and

He will accomplish great things in and through you.

Years ago an ad claimed that Wonder Bread built strong bodies eight ways. I'm here to tell you that eight is not enough when it comes to God and what He wants to do in the lives of His kids. He wants to build you up in so many ways, you won't be able to count them. He wants to build your mind. He wants to build your body. He wants to build your emotions. He wants to build your spirit. He wants to make you strong in Him and in the power of His might, that He might reach through your life to an entire community that will perish apart from Him. And that's just for starters!

It all begins with your willingness to see yourself as He does—to allow yourself to be invested fully in the faith-building experiences He brings along the way. Why not believe that He really can accomplish in your life what He has set out to do?

God is not about to absent Himself from you. He will pour every bit of strength He has into you as His son and His daughter and enable you to become everything that He has designed you to be.

Because your Dad loves you, He builds you up.

CHAPTER NINE

My Dad Calls Me His Own

I once saw a cartoon of a middle-aged guy named Chester Crabtree that was at once humorous and depressing.

All of the kids in Chester's neighborhood decided to play football. Even though Chester was at home puttering around the house, somehow he got wind there was going to be a football game in a lot just a few blocks away. Despite the fact that he was in his mid-forties and sported a paunch, he decided it would be wonderful to play. He began reliving his high school days when he was a star player.

He rushed into his bedroom and got suited up—pads, jersey, pants, cleats, and even an old helmet. He was so excited he couldn't wait to mix it up on the lot.

He flew down to the sandlot and planted himself in the middle of the kids.

Chester didn't know it, but he looked out of place, even bizarre. He was the only adult. His belly hung over his football pants and his old jersey didn't fit. As the kids were staring at him, he was salivating, waiting for that moment when he could make his first hit.

Finally one of the kids stepped out off to the side and said, "Okay, I'll take Stuffy and Sloppy and Timmy and Joey and Patsy." "Yeah!" they all shouted and off they ran. Then another kid stepped out and announced, "I'll have Huey and Martha and Bumper and Tommy and Marian." "Yeah!" they said and ran off with him. Everyone screamed, rushed to the middle of the field, and began to play.

Everyone, that is, except Chester. Nobody had called his name. No one wanted him on their team. Still Chester stood there, waiting for his name to be called. The seconds turned into minutes, then hours. Still Chester stood there in his cleats and pads and helmet.

The last frame of the cartoon shows Chester under the glow of a street light. It's now dark and a police car is cruising up beside him with the officer radioing in to headquarters, "Looks like we've got another weirdo here, only this one is in a football uniform."

Many think that's a funny cartoon—unless they identify with Chester.

Maybe Chester is you. Maybe you were left out or rejected or overlooked. Perhaps you were the one who was never good enough to be picked for the team. When that happens in real life, it's not exactly hilarious. It can have agonizingly deep and long-lasting effects.

The Sting of Rejection

Consider a friend of mine named Jack. Childhood rejection deeply scarred him and altered his entire life. Let's allow him to tell his own story.

I'm the youngest son of a preacher, and I mean preacher in every sense of the word. My dad was not a teacher or a minister, but a preacher. I think his basic idea in raising us kids was that if he could not preach the devil out of us, then the only thing to do was to beat the hell out of us. Two of my sisters were sexually abused by him, and my oldest brother was routinely beaten and emotionally abused. As for myself, it started out with a leather strap and graduated to a closed fist.

But more damaging was the emotional side. As I grew older and older and the other kids fled home, the anger and discipline turned more and more toward me. From my earliest recollection I knew I was no good and could never be saved. I was just a bad seed, waiting to go to hell. I can still hear the phrase, "You're never going to amount to anything," every time I fail. I knew, at the young age of five or six, that I was going to hell. And I was reminded of this fact each and every time I did something wrong. For me there was no hope. This I knew deep down inside.

I left home at sixteen. Since I was going to hell anyway, I made up my mind to take as many others with me as I could. I then began my life of drugs and alcohol and anger. I dove into the darkest part of life that I could find. After fifteen years of wandering from state to state, and job to job, after two failed marriages and countless relationships, I ran to the hills and a life of solitude in the bottle.

It's pretty lonely when you feel as though nobody cares about you. It cuts deeply that nobody wants you or has a place for you.

A Slot of Your Own

What a wonderful and heart-warming discovery it is, therefore, to learn that because your Dad loves you, He calls you His own. Because He loves you, He has a special place just for you. More than that, He is so proud of you, He asks you to represent Him. And that's only the tip of the iceberg!

Peter explains the truth about all these things in 1 Peter 2:9. Be prepared to be awed!

But you are a chosen generation, a royal priesthood, a holy nation, His own special people, that you may proclaim the praises of Him who called you out of darkness into His marvelous light.

Because your Dad loves you, He calls you His own. It sounds great, doesn't it? But what does it mean?

First, it means that your perfect Dad gives you a very special place. He picks you out of the crowd and gives you a specific slot to slip into. He has reserved for you a distinct place in His family. That's what Peter means when he writes, "You are a chosen generation."

Peter's message wasn't new. He was simply reiterating what God has continually said through the course of His Word. In Exodus 19:5 God said about His people, "You shall be a special treasure to Me above all people." In Isaiah 43:20 God calls His people "My people, My chosen." Then in John 15:16 Jesus tells His people, "I chose you."

To catch the full significance of these statements you have to put them in perspective. Today it is not at all uncommon to feel rejected, as if nobody cares for you, that there's no place for you. Buddy knows exactly how that feels.

Buddy's upbringing was extraordinarily abnormal, but he didn't know it. It had always been that way for him; that's how he understood life to be. So there was nothing particularly unusual when, at five years of age, his mom and dad took him to visit a great aunt and uncle whom he had never met. They drove quite a distance to spend the day with this elderly couple. Buddy had fun playing in the big yard outside.

Finally, when he figured it was time to go home, he ran into the house—only to find that his parents had left hours before. They had chosen not to take him and had no intention of coming back for him. Naturally, that filled this little guy with mountains of insecurity and anxiety. Those feelings diminished somewhat several months later when his parents showed up again and took him home.

He breathed a sigh of relief—for awhile. A few months later it happened again. Only this time, his insecurity and anxiety had grown so deep that he couldn't shuck them off. For years he found himself wrestling with this demon of anxiety and insecurity. He couldn't help but feel that something awful was about to happen to him. It didn't make any difference that he masked his feelings by appearing jovial and having it all together. In the depths of the night he felt horribly insecure and undone.

Buddy is not that different from any of us. He simply desired to be wanted, to be needed, to feel as if there were a place for him and that somebody wanted him to occupy that place.

Thank God there is such a person! When God is your Dad, He truly meets this need. One of the most basic things He wants you to know is that He loves you so much, He has a special place in His family just for you. He chose you before you even knew Him and He asked you to become a part of His family. It doesn't make any difference what anyone has said to you, nor does it matter how you feel about it. He urgently wants you to know that because He loves you, He gives you a special place.

If you're having trouble believing this, I find it's amazingly helpful to go back and read aloud the statements He has made time and again about you:

"You shall be a special treasure to Me above all people."

"You are My people, My chosen."

"I chose you."

Never forget! Because God loves you, He has a very special place for you.

A Starring Role Just for You

Second, because God loves you, He has a special role for you to play. He asks you to represent Him. Peter used language his contemporaries would understand when he called them "royal priests." "You are a chosen generation," he wrote, "a royal priesthood."

During the time of Peter, priests had a twofold function. On the one hand, they were to represent people to God. On the other hand, they were to represent God to people. However you shake it down, they were peculiarly God's representatives. When people saw them they were supposed to be able to see the Lord.

Allow yourself to imagine what that might mean. Do you realize its significance?

If your perfect Dad asks you to represent Him, that means He believes in you, He trusts you, He's proud of you. It means He's not worried that you might foul up or do something to embarrass Him. I think that's pretty amazing. Every parent knows what it's like to be embarrassed by his or her child.

Some years ago my wife and I went to a school program where each class did its own presentation. One class would come up to the stage and sing its songs, then sit down on the front steps. Then the next class would come up, sing, and be seated. And so on.

I don't know who arranged the schedule, but the kindergartners started the program. Their teacher had allowed two particularly rambunctious boys to stand together in the front row. During their presentation they were perfect gentlemen. They sang their songs and smiled and earned the best audience response you could hope for. These were fun, full-of-life kind of kids. When they finished doing their number they sat down along with the rest of the group.

Then the first grade came up. They did their number and got through it just fine. But by the time the second grade got up, these two little guys were getting tired of this nonsense. So one nudged the other, who

145

let it go . . . for a few minutes, anyway. Until he leaned over and pushed his friend. That was no big deal until the first elbowed the other one right in the ribs—popped him a good one. The second one wasn't about to let that go, so he waited until he thought no one was looking and then really jammed his friend a good one. That wasn't so bad until the first turned and spat on his sidekick. Naturally, the second one couldn't let that go, so he slugged his friend. And that's when things really fell apart.

Up until that point, the teacher had been unaware of any of this. When it first started, of course, someone in the crowd chuckled. Next you heard an outright laugh. And by the fifth or sixth altercation, a ripple of laughter was spreading across the whole crowd. Eventually the teacher realized what was taking place and hustled her boys off the front row and out of the room. We didn't see them again.

The whole episode was quite funny—unless one of the delinquents was related to you, as was the woman seated next to my wife. As she watched her son spit on the boy next to him, I think she wanted to dematerialize. She yearned to be any other place in the world but in that audience. She wished somehow that her son had never come into that room, had never participated in school. No doubt she imagined him at that moment at home, bound and gagged.

If you're a parent, you know what it's like to be embarrassed by your kids, don't you? I'll bet you stay away from certain situations because you know what happens if you don't. You know what your little people will do.

When my own kids were little and we decided to eat in a restaurant, I always asked the same question.

As the waitress came to take our order, I'd automatically turn to my kids and ask, "Okay, what do you want to spill?"

That is why it so amazes me to think that although God knows His kids through and through and perfectly realizes they might do something to embarrass Him, He still asks them to represent Him. He not only desires it, He encourages it. He invites them to go out and proclaim His praises, as it says in 1 Peter 2:9: "The praises of Him who called you out of darkness into His marvelous light."

It's possible you might question God's judgment on this issue. You may believe that the very last thing you could do would be to represent Him. You might feel as though your life is so messed up it simply wouldn't be possible for you. You're so crushed by your failures, so stymied by your shortcomings, that you don't see any way you could represent God adequately. Perhaps, after long years of hard work and faithfulness, God might ask you to represent Him—but not now.

Is that what you think? If you do, you're mistaken. That isn't the way God works. When He is your Dad, because He loves you, He gives you a special role. He calls you to be His representative wherever you are. Right now. No questions asked.

Ambassador Brent

Several years ago I met a young kid named Brent. Brent started using drugs with his dad when he was three years old. You can imagine the tone such a habit set for his life. He finally left home at twelve years of age after a particularly vicious fist fight with his dad.

By the time he was fourteen, somehow he entered into a relationship with God. God introduced

147

Himself to Brent through another kid. Instantaneously, Brent realized that he had a Dad who loved him absolutely. He knew he had a Dad who called him His own. He had this sense that he had been given the opportunity to go out and represent his perfect Dad.

Forget for a moment that this young man's hair hung down below his knees. Forget that he was a bizarre-looking kid with earrings everywhere you can imagine. Forget that he was far from being mature in his faith or even in his life. It made no difference. He was so excited about this relationship and so thrilled with his new life that he ran around blurting out the news to everybody he met. And would you believe it—within a few weeks he had introduced others of his friends to this Dad who would love them forever!

The truth is, representing your perfect Dad has little to do with the struggles of your life. It has everything to do with the *Dad* in your life. When God is your Dad, because He loves you, He has a very special role for you. He loves to have you represent Him to other people.

Stylin' for the Lord

Third, because your Dad loves you and calls you His own, He gives you a special style. He changes your life so much that suddenly, probably for the first time, you stand out from the rest of the crowd in a positive way.

When Peter calls God's people "a holy nation," he means their lives are unique. They live differently from everyone else. The word *holy* means "set apart." It means "different." It means "peculiar." It means "unique." Peter declares that when people have a new life in God, everything changes—their values, their behavior, their language, their goals, even their appearance. Everything about their life changes because of their relationship with God.

For vastly more people than you might think, this truth seems too good to be true. The years have taken such a toll on them that they find it enormously difficult to believe they could ever extricate themselves from the past. They think their lives have been stained so deeply and this soiling has worked itself so far down that there's no way to root it out. They can't believe they have the opportunity to start fresh.

But Peter took pains to tell us that such an opportunity *does* exist. When you enter into a relationship with God as your Dad, *everything* changes. You really do start fresh.

You say you want proof? Then meet Lucy.

Lucy had a horrible childhood. She was molested repeatedly as a little girl. Finally, when her mom became aware of what was happening, Lucy was shipped off to live with relatives. She hadn't been there very long when it started all over again. The head of the household began sexually abusing her. By then, though she was not yet even a teenager, Lucy took off to live on the streets.

It doesn't take a lot of imagination to realize what happens to a pre-teen living on the streets. She was raped several times. She got involved in everything you can imagine—booze, drugs, crime, anything depraved. Who among us would have looked at her and predicted she had much of a future?

Your opinion would change radically, however, if you could meet Lucy today.

She's an entirely different person—in fact, she's one of my favorite people, one of the sweetest individuals I know. She is one of the most loving, encouraging, warm, positive folks I have ever met. She is fun to be around. She's lightens up your day. She makes you feel that life is worth living and that whatever your struggles might be, they aren't as bad as you thought they were. Everything about her style belies her upbringing.

What happened? She entered into a relationship with God as her Dad!

When God became her Dad, instantly she was given a brand new life. She had been washed clean. Now she was whiter than snow, and whatever stained her past no longer existed. She could start all over with a brand new song on her lips.

Does this sound too good to be true? Does it sound like Fantasy Land? If you're like many people I talk to every day, I know you may be struggling with all of this. If you are, may I suggest that you meditate on two verses? One is 2 Corinthians 5:17: "If anyone is in Christ, he is a new creation; old things have passed away; behold, all things have become new." Psalm 40:3 is another good one: "He has put a new song in my mouth—praise to our God."

Take the time to rehearse these two verses. When you do, it should become clear that starting a new life with God is exactly that: *new*. Brand new. It's fresh. It's clean.

And it's just for you. Your Dad loves you so much that He gives you a special style.

Heaven Needs No FDIC

Fourth, because your Dad loves you, He calls you His own and gives you a special security. When God is your Dad, you belong to Him and to Him alone.

Peter calls God's children "His own special people." That's saying a mouthful. Literally this phrase is, "a people that has become His possession." That reflects closely what Paul says in 1 Corinthians 6:20 where he tells his Christian friends they were "bought with a price." Do you know what that price was? The very blood of Jesus Christ.

God so loved you that He gave His one and only Son that as you believe in Him you might not perish, but have life. He bought you with the price of His own Son. When He takes you into His family, you are His. There is nothing and no one who can take you away from Him.

Many of us lose sight of this truth far too easily. So quickly we take our eyes off of our heavenly Father. We know all too well what Paul was talking about in Romans 7:18-19: "For I know that in me (that is, in my flesh) nothing good dwells; for to will is present with me, but how to perform what is good I do not find. For the good that I will to do, I do not do; but the evil I will not to do, that I practice."

It's precisely because it is so easy to lose sight of this that God reminds us time and again that when you are His, you are His forever. You belong to Him and to Him alone.

Folks, if that's not security, I don't know what is.

Sure, we live in a world where it is easy to feel overlooked, left out, rejected. Maybe your childhood underscored that for you and it's difficult for you to get beyond it. Maybe the experiences that marked both your childhood and your adult years have made it difficult for you to believe that anybody could truly care about you or have a special place for you.

Whatever your story, you must understand that when you come into a relationship with God as your Dad through Jesus Christ, all bets are off. At that point, you enter into a whole new reality. God says this in so many ways throughout the Bible that it is tough to avoid. But hearing it is not enough; you must begin to live it. Until you do, it won't make a dent in your life (let alone in anybody else's).

Puppet Porters to Paradise

Yesterday I received a postcard from a good friend of mine who for years has ministered to people through puppets. She goes to little churches where others don't seem to want to waste their time. When I got the card she was visiting Northern California.

In one little town lived a young woman named Rosa. Rosa had five children, no spouse, no outside support, and had lost all hope—so much so that she had decided to take her life. I don't know how, but somebody got Rosa to come to my friend's puppet show at a tiny hole-in-the-wall church in Rosa's town. And that night, through the ministry of my friend and those silly puppets, Rosa came to understand that God loved her. Finally she heard that she had a Dad who cared about her.

Instantly, everything in her life changed. She realized her life wasn't over. She understood she didn't have to throw it away. She saw that God had a whole new thing out there for her to do. Simply because God loved her, she could be a whole new person.

She got so excited about this that she showed up the next night with a few of her neighbors. Well, more than a few. Fifty-nine, to be exact. Several of those fifty-nine had the joy of entering into a new life as well.

Now, be honest with me. If God could call Rosa His own (and He did!), couldn't He call you His own as well? And if God could use Rosa—a woman who was ready to commit suicide, a woman who believed her life was over—within hours of her being adopted into His family, isn't it possible that God could use you, too?

Your perfect Dad has a special place for you. He is excited that you are going to represent Him. He will never allow anyone to tear you out of His hands.

His invitation has been delivered. Your name is on it. It's in your grasp.

What do you say?

Because your Dad loves you, He calls you His own.

CHAPTER TEN

My Dad Gives Me Freedom

It's surprising how many people think of God as a giant lawgiver—a judge, a policeman, a drill sergeant. They assume God's greatest desire in life is to control them and to so arrange their circumstances that they're forced to do whatever He wants them to do.

In one way, I suppose their error isn't so surprising. There is no question some earthly fathers fight the urge to control their kids . . . and in a number of cases, lose the battle. Like Clair's dad:

> I can't relate to all this talk about fathers who were absent or uninvolved in their daughters' lives. My father was over-involved in my life. I would have given anything for some freedom from my father when I was growing up.

In fact, he's still over-involved in my life—dictating, smothering, controlling. My sisters and I call him little Hitler behind his back. I need a break from that man.

You may well have had a dad like that. He may have held you so tightly that he almost strangled you. He may have throttled the very one he wanted to help to thrive. Over the course of your lifetime, perhaps he has made you bitter or angry or resentful. Or maybe to this day you feel helpless because you were never allowed to try your own wings. It may even be that your dad's conduct has affected how you understand the way your perfect Dad wants to operate in your life.

If that's true of you, let me tell you something you may not know about God. As your Father, He gives you an immense amount of freedom. He loves to give His kids freedom. He always has. Just look at His track record.

A Famous Story Misnamed

One of the Bible's best-known stories illustrates this beautifully. Luke 15:11-24 is the famous parable of the prodigal son. But I think it has been misnamed. It would much more appropriately be called the parable of the loving father. At the heart of this story you discover what it means for a dad to give his kids real freedom and thereby express true love.

Here's how Jesus told the story:

A certain man had two sons. And the younger of them said to his father, "Father, give me the portion of goods that falls to me." So he divided to them his livelihood. And not many days after, the younger son gathered all together, journeyed to a far country, and there wasted his possessions with prodigal living.

But when he had spent all, there arose a severe famine in that land, and he began to be in want. Then he went and joined himself to a citizen of that country, and he sent him into his fields to feed swine. And he would gladly have filled his stomach with the pods that the swine ate, and no one gave him anything.

But when he came to himself, he said, "How many of my father's hired servants have bread enough and to spare, and I perish with hunger! I will arise and go to my father, and will say to him, 'Father, I have sinned against heaven and before you, and I am no longer worthy to be called your son. Make me like one of your hired servants.' "

And he arose and came to his father. But when he was still a great way off, his father saw him and had compassion, and ran and fell on his neck and kissed him. And the son said to him, "Father, I have sinned against heaven and in your sight, and am no longer worthy to be called your son." But the father said to his servants, "Bring out the best robe and put it on him, and put a ring on his hand and sandals on his feet. And bring the fatted calf here and kill it, and let us eat and be merry; for this my son was dead and is alive again; he was lost and is found."

When God is your Dad, because He loves you, He gives you freedom. Let's explore what this means.

A Desire God Put There

First, understand that God Himself placed within you a strong desire to be free. He designed you to be free. More than that, He knows that your maturity is a function of your freedom; you can't have the one without the other. He wants you to discover, on your own, that the only way to find true freedom and real life is by trusting Him and living in His love.

When Jesus' story opens, we see a young man chomping at the bit to be free. He feels completely hemmed in at home and is straining to break free.

To fully understand what's going on here, some background might be helpful. Jewish law stipulated that a father with two sons would bequeath his entire estate to both boys. The first son would receive two-thirds while the younger son would inherit the rest. Normally, as the father got up in years, he would transfer ownership of his estate to his sons. While they would legally own it, he would continue to receive all of the income from it until he died. After his death the sons would own the estate as well as all the income derived from it.

What the boy in Jesus' story was asking, then, was not all that unusual. The only unusual aspect was the timing of his request. He didn't want to wait until his father had passed from the scene. He coveted not only the estate, but the income derived from it.

This young guy thought there was a whole lot more to life than he had experienced. He believed if he could just break free from the prison that had entrapped him for so many years, he would be far happier. If he had the bucks to make possible the lifestyle he wanted, he would really score. That's what precipitated his request. If he had the cash to fund his ideas, life would be a blast!

Now, don't get the wrong idea. Don't assume there was something devious about this young man. There really wasn't. All he wanted was the opportunity to try life on his own. He had come to the point where he wanted to test his wings. And in this case he acted on that desire to the hilt.

Can anyone fail to relate to the young man? Is there anybody who, at one point or another, has not had the simple desire to break free?

I think the passion of the prodigal is the passion of every heart that says, "I want to be free. I want to be who I am. I want to be able to grow up and I don't see how that's possible if you continue to thwart my decisions and get in my way. So I would appreciate it if you would move aside and let me seek the life I know is waiting for me out there. Just let me at it—I know that if I can do this thing my way, it's going to be so much better."

Freedom to Fail

Ruth Graham, the great evangelist's wife, once wrote about one of her own prodigals. She addressed her poem to God:

> For all who knew the shelter of the fold,
> its warmth and safety and the shepherd's
>   care
> and bolted,
> choosing instead to fare out into the cold,
>   the night,
> revolted by guardianship, by light,
> lured by the unknown,

eager to be out and on their own,
freed to water where they may,
feed where they can,
live as they will,
till they are cured,
let them be cold, ill.
Let them know terror.
Feed them with thistle, weed and thorn
who choose the company of wolves.
Let them taste the companionship wolves
    give
to helpless strays.
But, oh, let them live.
Wiser, though torn.
And wherever, however far they roam,
follow and watch,
and keep Your stupid,
wayward,
stubborn sheep,
and someday,
bring them home.[1]

While a child's prodigal lifestyle worries parents, those growing into adulthood don't see it that way. They have yet to fully experience the hard knocks of life. They don't understand what's waiting for them out there. They think life is going to be so much more fun because they're the ones writing the script.

Are you ready for a shock? As the perfect Dad, God knows His kids want to be free. He wired them that way. If ever you felt that desire in your own life, God understands. It doesn't take Him by surprise. He knows how easy it is for the grass to appear so much greener on the other side of the fence. He knows that sooner or later you probably will want to try it out. He understands your desire to be free, because that's how He made you.

No Freedom, No Maturity

Second, your perfect Dad knows that maturity is a function of freedom. To a degree, the reverse is also true: real freedom is a function of maturity.

It was only as the prodigal experienced what he thought would be freedom that he discovered captivity. It was only then that he realized what he thought had been captivity was actually freedom. He could never have come to that conclusion without leaving home and trying life for himself.

The dad in Jesus' story displayed an incredible amount of trust and insight. He knew his son was making a colossal error in judgment. And he foresaw the huge loss, devastating pain, and anguish that awaited his son. Yet at the same time, he knew that his son would never grow up until finally he came to that conclusion himself.

So when his son came to him and asked for his inheritance and his freedom, his dad gave him what he wanted. He let him go. There's no hint of anger or bitterness or the exchange of cross words or the burning of bridges. You never hear him saying, "I'm telling you right now, buster, if you leave now, don't bother coming back. If you try it your way you are going to fall flat on your face. And when you splatter I don't want to see you come crawling back to me. The door will be bolted. The minute you leave I'm changing the locks. So go ahead—try it, if you think you're man enough."

Nowhere in the story do we see the man react that way. To the degree he was able, he met his son's desires.

No doubt we can guess what his feelings were. He must have felt sad, frustrated, and a little rejected. He worried about what was about to happen and where this decision would take his beloved son. Nevertheless, he meets the desires of his son's heart.

Don't misunderstand. He didn't give his son something that wasn't rightfully his. He had already set aside one-third of his estate for this young man, so even though it was unusual timing, the inheritance still belonged to his son. And despite the fact that his son's departure would change things at home, this dad met his boy's desires.

From Hog Heaven to Just Hogs

And what did the son do? He took everything he had and plowed it directly into pleasure. Truth to tell, this young guy wasn't free at all. He was captive to his glands, to his greed, to his grandiose ideas about what lay ahead. He did it his way—and lost everything he had in no time flat.

What the son did today is called, "prodigal living." That word "prodigal" means wasteful, undisciplined, wanton, unrestrained, unchecked. It sure fits this guy. He blew everything he had.

I doubt he ever realized his treasure was slipping away. He was so caught up in the magic of the moment, he didn't notice that his bankroll was running dry. And so he partied hearty, the good-time Harry of the region. He not only spent on himself, but he spent on everybody else. He was having a great time . . . until he had squandered the ranch.

By the time the smoke cleared, there was nothing left. It hadn't evaporated overnight, but it came as a shock to him. He woke up one day and found nothing there. No food. No funds. No friends. He didn't even have the same kind of future that just months before was certain to be his. It had seemed like so much fun—and now he had to think about little things like survival.

I love the way that one preacher, years ago, wrapped up this story. About this young man he said, "He went to the dogs, lost all his togs, and slept with the hogs."

I don't think there could have been anything more humiliating or embarrassing for a young Jewish man. It would have been detestable to him to have to feed pigs. Yet, that's where he ended up. And as if that weren't bad enough, not only did he have to feed them, but he didn't even have enough food for himself.

He had hit bottom. Everything had vanished. His "freedom" had left him in far worse condition than any "prison" he thought he had at home.

Insight from a Pig's Trough

It was only when he was forced to room with swine that he began to see things differently. It was only now that he saw reality as it really was. It was only when he came to envy his bacon-bits pals that he realized his "captivity" had actually been freedom and that what he thought was "freedom" was actually captivity.

It's not that different for you and me. And what is so astonishing to me is that your perfect Dad knows you need to be free to find true freedom. As your Dad, God knows that your freedom and your maturity are intertwined. You cannot gain one without experiencing the other.

Throughout your life, God has given you the ability and the freedom to follow after every one of your desires. He's never applied a stranglehold to you. He doesn't do that with His kids. You can go back as far as Adam and Eve and you won't find any exceptions.

God loved Adam and Eve with all His heart. He created them to be perfect and a part of that perfection was freedom. He gave them the opportunity to be free, to make their own choices, to manipulate their environment however they desired. Although He told them what it would take to make them happy, He gave them the freedom to decide whether that's what they wanted to do. Unfortunately, they chose poorly.

Some people don't believe this. These critics point to a man like Jonah and say, "Well, there's one who God controlled. Look at how He directed the fish to swallow that guy so He could force him to do what He wanted him to do." But think about it this way. If that fish hadn't swallowed Jonah, he would have drowned. When God sent Jonah to the belly of the fish, He was giving His child extra time to make some decisions about his life. That's not controlling; that's grace.

Even Jesus had the opportunity to decide against God's plan for His life. He knew what lay ahead. He knew the meaning of crucifixion. He knew all about torture and anguish and the agony of losing those who were closest to Him. He knew what it would be like to see His friends turn their backs on Him and walk away.

So when Satan came to Him in the wilderness and said, "Man, you don't have to go through all of this. Listen! I've got a better way. I'll make You king for a day. I'll make You the head of this whole world and You won't have to go through any of it. Just walk my way." Jesus could have chosen that option—but He didn't. Thank God He didn't!

God's Word teaches consistently that our perfect Dad gives His kids freedom. He wants any relationship with Him to be a function of desire and not of enforcement. He gives you the freedom to follow your heart—for better or for worse.

Tough Lessons

Please don't miss an important principle implicit in all of this. God knows that sometimes it is only when you experience the worst that you will desire the best. That's why He allows you the freedom to make decisions that He knows are bad. If a person never has to deal with the consequences of dumb decisions, how are they ever going to learn to make good ones?

It is of little value to constantly bail somebody out of jams they've created for themselves. That only robs them of the experiences they need to grow up. Anyone who has dealt with an alcoholic knows what I mean. It is of no value to force an alcoholic to dry out—to plead with him, to beg him, to cajole him, to fix things for him. Until he finally hits bottom and has to deal with the awful consequences of bad decisions, he will never be committed to the change demanded over the long haul.

God operates with His kids on the same basis. He loves you so much, He gives you a phenomenal amount of rope—enough to hang yourself. But His wager is that, slightly before you choke, you will call out to Him and say, "Hold it! Wait a minute! Maybe there is a better way."

Your perfect Dad loves you so much that He gives you enough freedom to become mature.

This Way to True Freedom

Third, your perfect Dad knows you will find true freedom only as you trust Him with your life and begin to live simply in His love.

That's what the prodigal found out. When finally he hit bottom, he realized how truly loving and secure and peaceful his home had been. He had come to understand that the world can be a chillingly cold place. Unforgiving. Harsh. When the chips were down, no one stepped forward to truly care.

Would this young man ever have come to such a realization apart from his hard experience? No. That's why his dad let it happen. But when the boy came to the end of the line, he saw what a tremendous mistake he had made and what a wonderful life he had enjoyed in his dad's love.

He felt terrible about rejecting everything his dad had given him. He couldn't believe he deserved his dad's acceptance, let alone his love. He had hurt him so deeply! He had taken his dad's love and thrown it in his face, turned his back on him and walked away. Why should his dad continue to love him? At best, the boy reasoned, he could go back to his dad and become a day laborer. Eventually, perhaps, he could apologize and show through his actions that his remorse was genuine.

He'd thrown away a wonderful life—and for what? A few months of parties and a shallow, hollow existence that led to nothing but death. So with his tail between his legs, feeling as low as he could possibly feel, he slinked home ready for the worst.

He was utterly unprepared for his extravagant reception.

His dad had never stopped loving him. As the chastened young man took the last few dusty steps toward home, his dad saw him, rushed to his son with arms opened wide, embraced him, drew him to himself, kissed him, and shouted to his servants, "Bring out the best robe and put it on him. Put a ring on his hand and sandals on his feet. Bring the fatted calf and kill it. Let's eat and be merry; for this my son was dead, and is alive again. He was lost and is found." Without so much as a moment's hesitation, in love this dad swept up his son and offered him the chance to live life as it was meant to be lived. Wow!

The Prodigal and You

When God is your Dad, you can expect the same kind of treatment. God is not some sort of divine puppeteer. He's not going to inflict His will on you. He's not going to force you to do things His way. Certainly, He gives you directions in His Word. But He then allows you the freedom to decide what you want to do. He gives you the freedom to choose to live life the way you think it ought to be lived—but He won't shield you from the consequences.

As your Dad, God gives you unfathomable amounts of freedom, perhaps even more than you think you can handle. He gives you the freedom to make your own mistakes and the freedom to live with the consequences of those mistakes. He gives you the freedom to learn that it is only in His arms and in His love that you will ever find true freedom and security and peace. When you finally realize how very much your heavenly Father loves you, He trusts that you will understand all of this and will then come to Him on your own.

He wants you to know that He understands your desire to be free. He is there when you come to Him, welcoming you with open arms no matter where you've been, no matter what you've done. He's ready to forgive you your failure, to help you enjoy a rich and full life. He wants you to know that as you nestle down into His love and into His life, not only are you going to find freedom from emptiness and ruin, but you will also find real security and a peace that cannot be stolen.

As you trust God as your Dad, you'll find that those "awful old directions" in the Word aren't there to block your fun. They are there to bless your heart! The directions in His Word have been placed there to build you up. As you learn and follow His truth—and only then—real freedom and joy will be yours.

Because your perfect Dad loves you so much, He gives you freedom. Freedom to fly. Freedom to die. Freedom to succeed. Freedom to fail. Freedom to turn your back on Him or freedom to rush into His arms opened wide for you in love. And I confess it makes me wonder: Where is that freedom taking you?

Take His gift and use it well. Your perfect Dad wants the very best for you.

Because your Dad loves you, He gives you freedom.

Note

1. Ruth Bell Graham, "For All Who Know the Shelter of the Fold," *Prodigals and Those Who Love Them* (Colorado Springs, Colo: Focus on the Family Publishing, 1991), 15.

CHAPTER ELEVEN

My Dad
Never Gives Up
on Me

Do you know what it's like to have somebody so committed to you that he is there for you no matter what? He never gives up on you. He's always there for you. You can bank on it.

I know a lot of people who would have given anything for such a relationship, especially while they were growing up.

Linda is a case in point. She began life as her daddy's only daughter. She was his princess. He extended to her every kind of love, encouragement, and affirmation that you can imagine. Father and daughter were inseparable. Wherever you found him, you found her.

Linda's dad loved to race automobiles. From the

time she was a little tyke he would take her with him to the track. By the time she was four or five she could already sling around terms like camshafts and trannies. She knew all of the grease monkeys by name and where they hung out on the track. She delighted in going there with her dad and spending time with his friends.

Often they would arrive early in the morning when racing teams were getting ready for the day. Generally there would be some kind of a break when everyone would traipse over to a favorite restaurant close to the track. Linda would get a cup of cocoa and a maple bar and would snuggle into her dad's shoulder. Big, burly guys would remark on what beautiful blue eyes she had. And she'd smile back at them and say, "Well, they're just like my daddy's." And they were.

Hers was a storybook existence . . . until she was seven years old. Then, overnight, her world turned upside down.

Doctors found an aneurysm in her dad's brain that sent him to a hospital for a series of surgeries. He drifted in and out of the hospital for more than a year. By the time he was allowed to go home, he was a changed man. Never again would he be the person his daughter had grown to love.

For ten years until he died, he suffered escalating seizures and mood swings that spiraled down by the day. This once jovial, fun-loving, affirming dad became increasingly hostile and emotionally abusive. He was violent and possessive, jealous, unpredictable, irrational, angry. Though for seven years he had doted on his daughter, he slowly began to direct all of his wrath her way.

Linda's mom now had to support the family. She

170

always held down at least two jobs, sometimes three. That meant the responsibility for caring for the house fell upon Linda. Even though she was still a little girl—nine, ten, eleven years old—she had to make sure that everything ran smoothly. In addition to that, she became her dad's primary caregiver.

Due to his failing emotional state and his mental instability, Lisa's dad increasingly vented his wrath. It seemed like she could never do enough to please him. Everything she did was always wrong. He constantly belittled her and chipped away at her self-worth. When finally he began to sexually abuse her, she thought she deserved it. After all she was, like he said, "just a piece of trash."

The nightmare continued until his death when she was seventeen. It was the only way she could escape.

Linda's dad simply wasn't there for her during her formative years. Not only was he absent from her corner, he wasn't even on her side. When she most needed that one important person to be affirming, to be supportive, to help her through the confusing struggles that a teen faces, he was nowhere to be found. Linda would have given anything for a dad who would have been there for her—a dad who never would have given up on her as she gave up on herself.

A Dad Who Will Be There

It wouldn't surprise me if you can relate to this woman because your life mirrored hers. Perhaps when you needed somebody, nobody was there for you.

If you never had a relationship with a supportive dad, or if you don't have such a relationship right now, I want to suggest that you try God.

Stories throughout the Bible prove that He never gives up on His kids. These stories are so many and so varied that I couldn't begin to exhaust them. But let me choose just one such story to demonstrate what I mean. As you consider this story and apply its principles to your life, it can't help but make an unbelievable difference to your future.

Let me tell you about Elijah. His story begins in the seventeenth chapter of 1 Kings. Though the details of his life may differ from yours, the principles involved are identical. As we reflect upon his life, think about how God interacted with him and see what God is saying to you through his story. You'll find that because your Dad loves you, He never gives up on you. He certainly never gave up on Elijah, even though Elijah gave up on himself.

The Man from Nowhere

Elijah was a nobody from nowhere. The text says, "And Elijah the Tishbite, of the inhabitants of Gilead, said to Ahab. . . ." At least from the world's perspective, Elijah was a nobody. If you search Scripture to find this man's lineage, you're going to have a long search. His genealogy doesn't exist. He seemed to come out of nowhere. He was truly a nobody.

I doubt he was a nobody to his mom and dad. At least they must have cared for him. In fact, if you consider his name, you realize they had some very special ideas about what would happen with this little boy. The name *Eli-jah* means "the Lord is God" or "Yahweh is God." He was named to commemorate his parents' feelings for the One who was the center of their lives. It may be that because Elijah carried such a handle, God looked down on him and said, "Hmmmmm. I can use this young guy."

Out of nowhere, God seemed to grab him and put him into a significant situation. A nobody from nowhere. Yet, all at once, God gave this young man a position and some promises and a whole lot of power.

The position: To be God's spokesman to His people Israel. He was to take God's Word to His people through Ahab, the king of all Israel.

The promises: That God would be with him no matter what. Further, that God would use him to do some extraordinary things.

The power: All he had to do was watch and step out of the way, for God would do some remarkable and mighty things through his life—even when he didn't have any strength of his own.

A Divine Sales Job

God must be some kind of incredible salesman, because Elijah immediately jumped into the role God asked him to fill. You almost get the feeling that he stretched his suspenders and said, "Hey—I can get into this!" So he took off on his first assignment.

He marched boldly up to King Ahab and said, "I'm here representing the water department and it is my task to tell you that we are shutting off the H_2O. Furthermore, it is not going to be turned back on until I give the word." Then he wheeled around and walked out. Now, let's be honest. The real reason he wheeled around and walked out is because God said, "You better split or he's going to kill you!" So he bolted.

God told Elijah where to go next and promised him He'd meet all of his needs. Even though the world around him was suffering through drought and famine, Elijah had both water to drink and food to eat. God cared for him by means of a brook and some birds. He took him to the Brook Cherith and there gave him water. Then he commanded the ravens to bring him food.

When it was time to move to the next level of trust, God sent him to a widow in Zarephath. "You go there and I will provide for you by means of her," God told the prophet. Understand, God intended to provide for him by means of a woman who had no means. When he got to his destination and asked this woman for something to drink and eat, she said, "I'd love to give it to you, but I don't have anything myself. As a matter of fact, if I use this oil and flour that I've got left, that's it! There won't be anything left after that, for either my son or for me."

Elijah must have learned sales techniques from his perfect Dad, because his pitch to this lady was unbelievable. He said, "I know you're going to find this hard to believe, but if you will just make a cake for me, this flour which you have will never disappear. In fact, it will continue somehow to show up. In addition to that, the oil that is left will continue to be replenished. I know you're not going to believe this, but just trust me. I realize you don't know me, you've never seen my face, and you know nothing about me, but you need to trust me on this. God told me this is what's going to happen."

Somehow he got her to buy into the deal. She made the cakes out of her precious flour and oil—and still they weren't used up! Exactly what Elijah said would happen, happened. She used the flour, but it wasn't gone. She used the oil, and that didn't disappear either. The arrangement continued until the appointed time that God said, "Now we're going to bring the utilities back and you can go about life in a normal way."

Another Step of Faith

It looked as if Elijah's God had the whole thing wired. Everything was going great.

And then this poor lady's only son died.

She was beside herself with grief. But Elijah was beginning to see he had an astonishing channel to the God of all creation. "Tell you what," he said. "I'll just pray for the kid." So he went in, laid hands on this young man, and prayed for him. And lo and behold, God raised him from the dead. Fantastic!

You can imagine how God's stock soared in value in Elijah's life. After confronting the king of Israel, after miraculously being sustained with water and bread when everybody else was starving to death, after having been used to raise a young man from the dead— this guy's strength knew no bounds. He decided he was pretty much invincible. It was time to move to the next level.

So he took off, walked right into the chambers of Ahab himself and laid on him some sensational statements. First he told Ahab what a fool he was for having led Israel into idolatry. It was a horrible mistake and he would pay dearly for that mistake. The people of God had forsaken God and were now worshiping idols—and God was not exactly thrilled.

Second, Elijah dared Ahab to gather all of the people of Israel and all the prophets of Baal to the top of Mount Carmel. There they'd have a little contest. He himself, Elijah, would square off against all the prophets of Baal.

No doubt Don King would have loved to promote such a fight. Ahab must have thought, *This is a piece of cake. I can't lose on this deal! I'm going to have everybody there and they are going to watch this idiot get slaughtered before their very eyes. That's going to do nothing more than raise my stature in their sight.* So the king took up the challenge. He commanded all the people to show up.

They did and completely ringed Mount Carmel, all the way to the top. The prophets of Baal were standing on the summit with one lone man, Elijah, who was still feeling pretty foxy. With all of the hub-bub going on, Elijah quieted the crowd and began to speak: "How long will you falter between two opinions? If the LORD is God, follow Him; but if Baal, then follow him." The text adds, "But the people answered him not a word." It was absolute and total silence.

Elijah wasn't feeling quite so shy. He said, "All right, I've got a little game for you. Famous executions for five-hundred! The answer is, 'Four-hundred and fifty prophets of Baal.' What is the question?" Do, Do, Do, Do, Do, Do, Do.

Well, the music may have been different, but the people were so stunned they didn't know what to say. So the prophet said, "The question is, 'Who was slain for worshiping false gods?'" Then he had the prophets of Baal build a sacrificial altar with stones and wood. Next they were told to put a bull on top of it. Elijah intended to do the same thing, but he said, "Don't light that thing because we are both going to call upon our gods and whoever is able to consume that sacrifice will be the real God."

The prophets of Baal thought this was wonderful. They began to chant and spout their incantations and dance around. It says that the minutes turned into hours and nothing was happening, so they turned up the volume and speeded up their pace. They gashed themselves so that blood soaked the ground. They screamed out to their god. And yet nothing happened.

Finally, Elijah began to mock them. I love the way Ken Taylor stated this in the original version of *The Living Bible*: "About noontime, Elijah began mocking them. 'You'll have to shout louder than that,' he scoffed, 'to catch the attention of your god! Perhaps he is talking to someone, or is out sitting on the toilet, or maybe he is away on a trip, or is asleep and needs to be wakened!' " (1 Kings 18:27, TLB).

The prophet mocked them so sharply that finally the people began to see that this Baal worship was silly, that it was never going to work. The people turned their backs on the prophets of Baal and began to drift toward Elijah.

Heavenly Fireworks

The prophet sensed the spotlight had come up on him so he said, "All right, watch this!" Instead of merely calling on his God, he decided to turn up the heat. He dug a trench around his altar and invited some bystanders to pour water all over it. But that wasn't enough. He had them come a second time and pour more water on it. That wasn't enough! He had them come a third time and pour more water on it. (Something like a Houdini production.) The water was so high that it filled the trench completely.

Only at this point, when it was impossible for the altar to be lit even with a blowtorch, did he pray. "God," he said, "You better bail me out of this!" No, that isn't what he said. He said, "Lord God of Abraham, Isaac, and Israel, let it be known this day that You are God in Israel, and that I am Your servant, and that I have done all these things at Your word.

Hear me, O LORD, hear me, that this people may know that You are the LORD God, and that You have turned their hearts back to You again" (1 Kings 18:36-37). That was it. No screaming, no gashing, no blood. There was a moment of silence and every eye gazed upon that sacrificial altar.

Suddenly, fire fell from heaven. It not only consumed the burnt offering, it consumed the wood, the stones, the very dust of the earth as well as the water. Everything was vaporized. The people, as one, began to shout, "The LORD, He is God! The LORD, He is God!" Elijah replied, "You'd better believe it!"

Just then he ordered the prophets of Baal seized and put to death. Elijah was on a roll. He was smiling from ear to ear. He turned to Ahab and said, "Now, I'm going to turn the water back on." Soon after he prayed, dark, threatening storm clouds began to form. It got blacker and blacker. He said to Ahab, "You'd better beat it home, because if you don't, you're going to drown." So Ahab hopped in his chariot and fled for home.

Elijah was psyched by now. He was so high about what had happened that he slipped on his sneakers and took off running. You could just see him as he caught up to Ahab, passed the king, and ran all the way to Jezreel. It was incredible. He was just blowing the smoke off the barrel of his gun when everything fell apart.

From Bold to Beaten

As soon as Ahab returned home he told his wife what had happened. Now, Jezebel had to be some kind of "coming at you" lady. Her rage was so hot that even though Elijah got wind of her response by messenger, he melted. This woman told the prophet,

"Buddy, the sun is not going to set tomorrow before you are dead meat."

And Elijah, mighty Elijah—still wearing his championship belt with his sneakers still on—cut out and ran. He was scared to death.

If you were God, how would you have responded to this man? I would have said, "I can't believe this wimp! After everything I have done for him—what in the world does it take? Obviously, whatever it takes, he doesn't have it. We've seen some pretty amazing things here, haven't we? One after another. But has that impressed you? Noooooooo. One lady speaks one cross word to you and you fold up and run. Well, I'm finding somebody else."

The wonderful thing about God is, He didn't respond like that. Instead, He met Elijah right where he was and demonstrated His concern for him. He reminded him of reality, of who really was in control. Then He motivated him to get back into the flow of trusting God so that He could do some even more amazing things.

God never gave up on Elijah, even though Elijah gave up on himself.

How about You?

Let me ask you something. If God were to be your Dad, your heavenly Father, would He give up on you? Or would He always be there for you exactly when you needed Him?

If you allow yourself to take the principles in this story and apply them to your own life, I think you will find some pretty fantastic truths.

First, God always cares for His kids, even when

they are feeling down and out. When Elijah caved in, when he freaked out and fled, God met him right where he landed. He didn't judge him, He didn't condemn him. Elijah didn't need any of that. He already felt bad enough himself. He knew he had blown it. He was frightened, but now he was also afraid of what God might think. He didn't need judgment and condemnation. And that isn't what he got. What he got was God's clear-cut concern. God simply said, "What are you doing here Elijah? What's happening, man?"

That's the truth you and I need to hear when we feel down and out. If we are God's kids, He always cares for us. If you've ever found yourself in a dungeon of despair, you know how bad you feel. You think it's impossible that things could ever come together for you. You know how easy it is to condemn yourself. You know how easy it is not to be able to forgive yourself. You know how easy it is to believe there is no way God could ever again have a place for you.

Surely that's how Peter must have felt after denying Jesus three times. It must have ripped him apart to think that one minute he was declaring his absolute loyalty to Jesus and the next minute he was denying Him. How could the Lord ever forgive him? How could he forgive himself? Why would God ever desire to be related to him again—much less use him?

And yet the truth is, God is right there to meet you, to help you understand how much He cares for you. God always cares for His kids.

Second, God always reminds His kids of reality. As He does so, He lays open the lies that get in the way. God forcefully reminded Elijah who was in control. Jezebel's threat was without teeth. She may have had a bodacious bark, but she had no bite at all. Her teeth were false. Her threat against Elijah had no force because she was up against the Lord of Creation. Elijah simply needed to remember who this God was whom he served.

It is vital that you understand this, too. Remember Linda? I had the opportunity to chat with her a few days ago. We were talking about a variety of issues and she said to me, "Do you remember that letter that I wrote to you about my life, where I told you all of the struggles I had and the horrible things that happened? Now that you know all of those things about me, how do you feel about me? Am I disgusting to you? Am I repulsive?"

Her question ripped my heart out. I found myself saying to her what the Lord of creation wanted to tell her Himself: "Linda! God loves you with a love that will never quit. Neither He nor I find you disgusting or repulsive. As a matter of fact, because you are the child of a King, you are going to be a princess forever. Your Dad has determined that you have a unique place in His heart and in His Kingdom."

It is so easy to buy into the lies, to feel as though your difficult experiences have ended your life, to think there is no way you can ever get back up and get going again—and certainly not that God could ever use you.

But the Lord wants to remind you of reality. His reality is a universe apart from what the world might say to you. He is the Lord of Creation and when He is your Dad, He will do amazing things in your life.

Third, Elijah's life teaches us that God always challenges His children to reach for His best and then cheers them on as they go for it. Without so much as hinting at his frailty, God came back to Elijah as if nothing had happened. In fact, He addressed him with the same sentence that He began with, "So, what are you doing here, Elijah?" And without skipping a beat, He sent him on a brand new assignment. He told him, "We've got a lot to do. You ain't seen nothin' yet. Come on, let's go out and get back into the fun things in life." Elijah left that cave, destined to do brand new things for God.

God never gives up on His kids. He just doesn't. He always challenges us to move to ever-new heights of life with Him. All along the way as we reach out for those new things, He cheers us on. He wants us to experience everything that He has reserved for us. And He wants that for you, too.

Because your Dad loves you, He never gives up on you.

CHAPTER TWELVE

Is God
Your Dad?

This is the last chapter and I've got to be really clear about something. You are missing out big time if God is not your Dad. If God is not your Dad, if He isn't your heavenly Father, when you feel down and out and up against it, you probably are. If God is not your Dad and you feel all alone, no doubt it's true.

But when God is your Dad, you're never alone. He promises never to leave you nor forsake you. Nor are you down and out even when you feel like it, because He promises to clean you up and to set you free. That's why it is so critical that you ask God to be your Dad. He wants you to be His child and to know all the stability which that entails.

There is no reason to spend even one more day

without having God as your Dad. You may have been hurt. You may have been rejected. You may have been overlooked. You may have been abandoned or pushed off to the side by your earthly father. But as the Bible reveals so graphically, your heavenly Father is a whole different character. He is the Lord of Creation, and when He is your Dad, He has an all-new life for you, forever.

I simply can't close this book without finishing Kendra's story. Remember her? The one who was so terribly and painfully abused as a little girl? The one who felt that she could never be God's child because she was so repulsive, so dirty? Let me tell you what transpired in her life. You'll love it!

Kendra struggled for years with an inability to "connect" with God, yet she could not shake a deep longing to enter into a relationship with Him. Finally, in an effort to resolve this conflict, she began five years of intensive therapy. The process had nothing whatsoever to do with God. Pronounced "recovered," she ended that phase of her life and hoped the pronouncement was correct. But still she felt a gnawing hunger deep within that couldn't be satisfied. Not even the right buzz-words seemed to help.

That's when she turned to a "new age" church to get healthy. Since the members were supposed to be so positive in their thinking, surely this would resolve her problem! But it didn't.

Finally, one day she decided to step out of her comfort zone and return to a "fundamental" church, the very kind of congregation she had been introduced to as a child. She had heard people in the community talk of Crossroads and knew it was big enough to slip in anonymously, so she showed up one Sunday morning and sat as far back as she could get.

Even though she had always felt as though God couldn't accept her as His child, she surprised herself that morning and spoke to Him on the way into the church building. "Okay, God," she began, "I'm going to give you one more chance. If you really *do* care for me, if you really *do* want to have a relationship with me, show me that this morning!"

Imagine Kendra's shock when on that very Sunday I handed out the "dad" questionnaires! Someone was asking her to answer the very questions she had spent a lifetime wrestling with! Hardly able to contain herself, she rushed out of church, got in her car, drove home, and answered that questionnaire as quickly as her fingers would stroke the keys on her typewriter. She then scurried to the post office and mailed her answers to me.

I received her letter a day later and was so overwhelmed that I found it almost impossible to read anything else. How could someone do such things to a little girl? How could anyone in his most horrible nightmare think of such ways to hurt someone so precious? Her response so startled me and her candor so impressed me that I telephoned her that evening to see if her story were really true.

Although our conversation was cordial, something she said really rattled my cage. She laid on me one stupendous "heavy."

"I'm going to give God the duration of this study to see whether He really cares for me," she declared.

"Whoa!" I replied. "No pressure!" How would her challenge make *you* feel?

I admit, it made me terribly uneasy. I told God

He'd better do His job, because I certainly wasn't up to doing for her what needed to be done!

Kendra was as good as her word. She attended every one of the studies during Sunday morning worship. She involved herself in a ladies' Wednesday evening Bible study which dealt with the topic of the week. None of this was easy for her. None of it was done without suffering through raging torrents of fear and trepidation. But to God be the glory—she hung in there!

Week by week, God spoke to her in ways she had never heard before. Layer by layer He peeled away the dross and fear from her life. Finally, two weeks before the end of the series, she gave her heart to the Lord during the Wednesday night study!

She came to believe that God really did want to be her Dad. He *really* loved her. He *really* had a special place for her. He *really* wanted to heal her and release her from all her years of frustration and hurt. And as she fell into His everlasting arms, He drew her irrevocably to Himself.

Days afterward, basking in the warmth of her Dad's love, she wrote another poem. But this poem was different from anything she had ever written. It was a poem about a Dad who loved her! See if it hits you as hard as it hit me:

The Rescue

Once there was a lonely child who was terribly defiled

and

When she experienced the horrors and the shame, she felt wicked, evil, and unclean

and

With such unworthiness ingrained, it left a very ugly stain

and

For her, religion it did distort—until God became her punishment and enemy

and

Through many years of toil and struggle she did recover; at least in part, but she still had that very ugly heart

and

Even as she studied the New Thought Queen, she still could not come clean

and

Then one day, she was strangely drawn to a church similar to that of those terrible days

and

With a skeptic's heart she committed to attend—but she really thought she'd never mend

and

As Pastor Tom led the songs, the congregation did respond with praises to their MIGHTY AWESOME GOD

and

As Pastor Bill preached the PERFECT DAD, his words of wisdom fell upon a cold and lonely heart

but

With her anger she came face to face, blaming God for her father's disgrace and

As the weeks wore on, discouraged she did get, but was determined not to quit

and

Oh, Sweet Sisters—How they prayed!—and even washed her feet one day

and

With the washing of her feet, Satan took a second seat

and

Then one Sunday she awoke—a voice spoke:

"For all these weeks you have tried and tried,

surely for you HE did not die!"

but

Her commitment she did keep—and with this, the enemy feared defeat

and

As the pastor spoke on that special day, the Spirit moved—and with a jolt, the Master called her as His own

and

With this she prayed:

"ROCK OF AGES, RESCUE ME! YOUR BRAND NEW CHILD

I WANT TO BE! SET ME FREE!"

and

With these words the Spirit swooped—like Jericho those walls came down! And beneath the rubble, there He found that tiny soul that had been bound

and

As He gently loosed those chains, a multitude of tears arose—and He exposed:

"THAT ENEMY HAS TOLD YOU LIES—IT'S FOR YOUR TEARS

THAT I DID DIE!"

and

As He washed away those rocks, Living Waters did atone—as JESUS became her Cornerstone

and

As that enemy gave it one last try, those wise sisters recognized his disguise

and

With the taking of her first Communion she knew that God's love for her was no illusion

and

NOW SHE FEELS A VERY SPECIAL KIND OF CLEAN—AND WITHIN HER HEART A SONG DOES RING, SAYING:

"HARK THE HERALD ANGELS SING, GLORY TO THAT

OLD AND ANCIENT KING! THE ROCK OF AGES

RESCUED ME—ONCE A CAPTIVE, NOW I'M FREE!"

Oh, what a joy it is to see the reality of God's new life bloom in someone's life! What a blessing to have a part in somebody coming to experience what it's like to be loved by the perfect Dad!

Please understand this: Kendra's story isn't one of a kind. Over and over again, God offers to be the perfect Dad to any who will receive Him. All it takes is entering into His family by believing in Jesus Christ. John says it so well:

> But as many as received Him, to them He gave the right to become children of God, even to those who believe in His name: who were born, not of blood, nor of the will of the flesh, nor of the will of man, but of God" (John 1:12-13).

God wants to be your Dad, your heavenly Father. Why don't you trust Him and allow that relationship to begin right now?

Why spend one more lonely moment apart from a perfect Dad who will love you? Just for the asking, you can have this most precious of all gifts.

Right now, right where you are, you can have a perfect Dad with a capital D—if you want one. He is the God of all creation. He stands with His arms open wide, inviting anyone who wants it to join His family, to become His son or His daughter. He stands with outstretched arms inviting you to come to Him through faith in His Son, Jesus Christ.

He wants to be what you've always wanted: A Dad who will love you.

STUDY GUIDE

Chapter One:
A Dad Who Will Love You

1. If you were to use just one word to describe your dad, what would it be? What if you had two or three more choices?

2. If you could go back in time and change your relationship with your dad, what would you change?

3. In as few words as possible, list the qualities of a perfect dad. Have you ever known anyone who embodied most or many of these qualities?

4. Recall that a *parataxic distortion* is "any attitude toward another person which is based on a fantasied or distorted evaluation of that person or on an identification of that person with other figures from

past experiences." Has your relationship with your own dad created any parataxic distortion in your relationship to God as your heavenly Father? If so, what?

5. Read John 10:30 and 14:6-9. What does Jesus say about His relationship to the Father? How similar is the Son to the Father? If you want to know what the Father is like, who should you observe?

6. Read Jeremiah 29:13. What must you do if you are to discover a new relationship with God as your Father?

7. Read Romans 8:14-17. According to verse 15, how are we freed from a spirit of fear? What new cry does God allow us to make? What promises does verse 17 make to you?

8. Read John 16:27. What does Jesus say about the relationship of the Father to you? How is this relationship established?

Chapter Two:
My Dad Accepts Me

1. What does "unconditional acceptance" mean to you? Did you feel this kind of acceptance from your own dad? Explain your answer.

2. Of the incidents from Jesus' life covered in this chapter (the Moral Zero, the White-Collar Robber Baron, the Social Outcast, the Public Health Hazard, the Tramp, the Blind Man, and the Thief), which most clearly demonstrates to you the unconditional acceptance of Jesus? Why? How did Jesus show God's unconditional acceptance?

3. Read John 8:1-8. How did God react to the woman with the problem?

4. Read Romans 5:8. Does it apply to you? If so, how? If not, why not?

5. Read Isaiah 1:18. What does this verse have to say about God's unconditional acceptance?

6. Read John 6:35. What must we do to avoid being spiritually hungry or thirsty?

7. Read Romans 8:38-39. According to this passage, what things can separate us from the love of God? What does this say about His unconditional acceptance?

8. What does the Bible tell us about God's willingness to accept us if we have struggles *after* we enter into a relationship with Him? How does 1 John 1:8-9 speak to this?

Chapter Three:
My Dad Guides Me

1. Describe the guidance you received from your dad as a child. Did it prepare you for the life you now live?

2. What is guidance? Where can you find it today?

3. Is guidance always positive and easy, or can it sometimes be difficult to follow? Describe such a time in your life.

4. According to the Bible, in what ways does God guide you? How open are you to this? Explain your answer.

5. Can you recall a time when you received guidance but rejected it, only to find out later that your response was a bad decision? Describe the circumstances.

6. Read Matthew 7:7-11. How does this relate to the value of our Dad's guidance in our lives?

7. Read through Psalm 1. What does this tell you about the guidance of your Dad in your life?

8. Proverbs 1 is a beautiful illustration of your Dad's guidance. What does it say to you about your Dad's desire for you and the importance of His guidance in your life?

Chapter Four:
My Dad Corrects Me

1. Describe the kind of discipline and/or correction you received as a child. What effect did it have on you? How has it affected you across the course of your life?

2. Have you ever heard the phrase, "This is going to hurt me more than it will hurt you"? What does it mean? Do you believe it ever to be true? Explain your answer.

3. Discuss the phrase, "Whom the LORD loves, He chastens." How have you experienced the truth of this in your own life?

4. Proverbs 12:1 features a close connection between correction and instruction. What is that connection? Have you learned how to handle correction in your own life? How might you need to work on this?

5. Matthew 16:21-23 tells an intriguing story that reveals a form of discipline exercised by Jesus with a close friend. What was it? What was Jesus' intention? How does it relate to what He says in Revelation 3:19?

6. Those who are truly children of God will be corrected by their perfect Dad. How do you respond to this? Can you separate the way He corrects—understanding His clear-cut commitment to you and your growth—from whatever else you may have experienced earlier in your life? If not, how can you move toward such a separation?

7. Proverbs 22:6 admonishes us to "train up a child in the way he should go." Why are we told to do this? Where does correction and/or discipline fit in with this process? How does godly discipline help your

children in later life? How will the lack of it hurt them?

8. Proverbs 13:24 directly states the value of discipline. How is this supposed to work? Where does "discipline" end and "abuse" begin?

Chapter Five:
My Dad Provides for Me

1. When you were growing up, did you simply assume your dad would provide for you? Explain your answer.

2. What does it (or would it) mean for you to know that your Dad will always provide for you? How do you think He would demonstrate this to you?

3. Have you ever struggled with your perfect Dad's provision? Have you ever felt that He does a better job providing for others than for you?

4. In what way is 1 Peter 5:6-7 helpful in understanding your perfect Dad's commitment to provide for you?

5. Do you regularly trust your Heavenly Father to provide for your day-to-day needs, or do you reserve that kind of trust for the big things in your life? Explain your answer.

6. Think through the sweep of the Bible. Did the Heavenly Father provide for His children or didn't He? What does He want you to learn from the way He has provided for others?

7. Read and reflect on Psalm 37:25. What is David saying? How would you communicate this truth to someone else?

8. Review Philippians 4:6-7. How do we develop in our lives the *fact* of our Father's provision for us?

Chapter Six:
My Dad Protects Me

1. Can you recall a time when someone protected you from something (or someone) dangerous? How did it feel to know you were protected?

2. What are some of the things parents protect their children from? How do they provide this protection?

3. What are some of the ways your perfect Dad protects you?

4. Name some specific incidents in which you experienced your perfect Dad's protection. Have you ever found out about His protection "after the fact"? If so, describe the situation.

5. What is the relationship between God's protection and man's growth? If we suffer or hurt, does it mean He no longer cares for us? Why or why not?

6. Discuss 1 Corinthians 10:13. How are you to participate in God's protection yourself?

7. According to Romans 8:28, how does God use the hurtful things in our lives?

8. Is it either scriptural or reasonable to assume that Christians will be protected from everything hurtful? If so, why? If not, why not?

Chapter Seven:
My Dad Listens to Me

1. As you reflect on your own childhood, did your dad listen to you? Did he like to spend time with you, or did you feel as if you were imposing on him? How would you describe your dad's listening skills and interest?

2. Have you ever had trouble listening to and hearing any of your friends or family? What do you need to change so that you will listen, hear, and respond?

3. Read Isaiah 30:19. What does this verse say about the character of God and His desire to listen to you? How will He respond when He hears you?

4. Exodus 16:8 reminds us that God hears things we may not even want Him to hear. How does this verse challenge you, specifically in regard to what you say? (Also compare Luke 12:3 and Malachi 3:16.)

5. As you reflect on Psalm 34:17, what is presupposed about the character of the one to whom God listens? Does this verse suggest any changes that you need to make? If so, what are they?

6. Read Psalm 50:13-16. According to verse 15, when you find yourself in trouble, what does God want you to do? What does He promise to do in response? How are we to respond to what He does? In what way does verse 16 describe a "kink in the phone line"?

7. Read 1 Peter 3:7. Is it possible for things to get between you and your Heavenly Father so He can't or doesn't hear you? Describe these things.

8. What does 2 Chronicles 7:14 have to say about talking to God and how He responds? What must we do to keep that communication line completely open?

Chapter Eight:
My Dad Builds Me Up

1. How can a parent build up a child? Did you experience this yourself while growing up? Explain your answer. According to the Bible, what are some of the ways in which your Heavenly Father builds you up?

2. Think about the various people Jesus encountered. Did He ever turn anyone away because of some problem they had? Describe some of the people Jesus accepted and affirmed who would have been difficult for you.

3. Jesus makes a radical statement in John 15:5. What does this mean for you? What has been your experience in this regard?

4. Read Acts 1:8. From what source does real strength come? How can you appropriate such strength?

5. Do you ever struggle with the idea that God truly loves, forgives, and accepts you? What makes you think He doesn't or couldn't? What would it take for you to accept Him at His word?

6. Read the story of Jesus and the woman at the well (John 4:1-30) or Zacchaeus (Luke 19:1-10). What do you learn about God's acceptance and affirmation from these stories? How does it apply to your life?

7. Read Genesis 50:20. What does this verse say about the means God uses to build up His kids? How has He done this in your life? What could you do to hinder this process?

8. Read John 10:10. What does this verse have to say about building you up? If you have not already done so, memorize this verse.

Chapter Nine:
My Dad Calls Me His Own

1. When you were growing up, did you ever feel as though your dad was proud of you? What did he do to give you that impression?

2. How important has your family name been to you? Was there ever a time you wished that you had a different name? Explain your answer.

3. What does it mean to be "called by God's name"? How basic is this to your own self-understanding?

4. In 2 Corinthians 5:20, Paul calls us "ambassadors of Christ." What does this mean to you? How does this relate to you?

5. Have you ever truly felt like "God's ambassador"? If so, describe a specific situation in which you acted as such. If not, what's getting in your way?

6. 1 Corinthians 6:20 tells us that God's people have been "bought at a price." What is that price? What are the implications of this purchase to you?

7. Read 1 Peter 2:9. What does this verse say about to whom you belong? How does this make you feel? How can you fully enter into the spirit of the passage?

8. Read 2 Corinthians 5:17. How do you become "a new creation"? What happens when you become a new creation? Is this true of you? Why or why not?

Chapter Ten:
My Dad Gives Me Freedom

1. When you were growing up, did your parents give you freedom? Did it increase as you got older? How did you handle the freedom you were allowed?

2. What does it mean to you to be "free"? How can freedom work both for you and against you?

3. Read John 8:31-32. What is Jesus trying to say? Does this have any significance for you? If so, what? If not, why not?

4. Do you believe God allows his children to be free? What does the Bible have to say about it? How does God show His commitment to His kids' freedom?

5. Read Galatians 5:1. What is Paul getting at? How does this relate to you right now?

6. Psalm 146:5-7 contains a powerful statement about freedom. Can you identify any area in your life in which God has set you free? Are there some other areas that you need to ask His help in?

7. Does being free mean you will suffer no consequences for bad decisions? If you have to face some difficulties due to poor choices, will God love you any less? Can you recall any episodes in the life of the apostle Peter that would help you in this regard?

8. John 8:34-36 contains an intriguing discussion about freedom. What applications can you see in this passage for your own life? How does your Dad give you freedom? How does His freedom enable you to grow?

Chapter Eleven:
My Dad Never Gives Up on Me

1. Describe a time in your life when you let somebody down. Was there ever a time when you let God down? If it seems to you as if you're the only one who has experienced this, refresh your memory by reading Psalm 51.

2. Do you know what it's like to have somebody "in your corner," especially when you're down? If you can, describe a situation in which you experienced this.

3. How do you think the disciples felt when Jesus was crucified? Do you think they felt vulnerable? Were they? Had God forgotten them or let them down? Compare Luke 22:60-62 with Mark 16:7 and John 21:15-19. Did Jesus give up on Peter? What does His treatment of Peter imply about His relationship with you?

4. Reflect on Philippians 1:6. What does this verse tell you about your perfect Dad's commitment to you?

5. According to Psalm 23, what is the heavenly Father's commitment to "being there" for His kids?

6. How easy is it for you to give up on God? Do you think it's possible that because it's easy for you to give up on God, you assume it's just as easy for Him to do the same to you? Read 2 Timothy 2:11-13. What does verse 13 have to say about this issue?

7. What do Jesus' words in Matthew 28:20 suggest about the depth of God's commitment to His kids?

8. Read Hebrews 13:5b. What is God's promise in this verse to you? How firm is it? What difference to your life would it make if you acted on it daily?

Chapter Twelve:
Is God Your Dad?

1. Is God your Dad? How do you know for sure?

2. Read Kendra's poem, "The Rescue," out loud. Does your life mirror any aspect of hers? If so, which ones? How does her poem make you feel?

3. Read John 1:12-13. What does this passage have to say about making God your Dad? Have you acted on this passage? If so, how? If not, why not?

4. Read Isaiah 55:1-2,6-7. Does this invitation sound appealing? How would God have you respond to it? What is He offering you?

5. Read Romans 10:9. What is the promise contained in this verse? What is your relationship to it?